Camille

C0-APH-034

Praise for Camille Cusumano's books

For *The Last Cannoli* (a novel)

> Attests to the power of storytelling to hold life together through all its diasporas.
>
> > —Lawrence Ferlinghetti, poet, venerable man of letters, City Lights Bookstore owner, and former San Francisco Poet Laureate

> *Cannoli* . . . is a lyrical, exuberant novel about an Italian American family facing an increasingly homogenized society.
>
> > —Laura A. Salsin, *Italian Americana*

For *Italy, A Love Story*

> Cusumano has put together an outstanding volume of women's travel writing, demonstrating a fullness of living. This collection is a page-turner.
>
> > —Carol Bonomo Albright, editor of *Italian Americana*

> When I first discovered Florence, with all the bridges except the Ponte Vecchio still destroyed, I fell in love. This proves the experience of loving Italy is not confined to women. But the women in this book offer a useful perspective, highly flavored, with engaging erotic implications . . . great voyeuristic fun.
>
> —Herbert Gold, author of *Haiti: Best Nightmare on Earth, Bohemia, Fathers,* and *A Girl of Forty*

In this thrilling and layered new collection, women . . . explore and describe in loving prose individual infatuations with a land that is both complicated by and adored for a rich tradition.

—*Sun Journal*

Camille Cusumano has assembled a unique cast of women writing about their encounters with Italy. Together, they come close to defining that indefinable something—the people, the culture, the fit of people and culture with their landscape—that draws the traveler again and again to this land.

—Lawrence DiStasi, Editor of
Una Storia Segreta, When Italian Americans
Were Enemy Aliens

A multi-faceted look at the charms of the popular Mediterranean country through the eyes of twenty-eight noted women writers. They contribute appealing personal stories of their travels to various parts of the country.

—*Santa Barbara News-Press*

For *Mexico, A Love Story*

Twenty-two distinctive and unique voices sweep the reader through an exhausting and passionate range of emotions. The book is alive with love and laughter, tears and tenderness, death—and voices from the spirit world. Reading it is like inhaling a culture in all its dimensions. Like the richness of

Mexico, the book sizzles with the heat and heart of the Mexican people and pulses through women in love.

—Rita Golden Gelman, author of
Tales of a Female Nomad

This insightful collection is filled with vivid descriptions and engaging characters. Women write about their love affair with Mexico and reveal a complicated lover imbued with beauty, passion, danger, and excitement.

—Rose Castillo Guilbault, author of
Farmworker's Daughter:
Growing Up Mexican in America

In this book, a love of Mexico flows from many springs. An L.A. teenager goes "home" to Oaxaca once a year. A woman goes on vacation and stays seventeen years. Some fall in love with colors, food, the sea; some discover themselves in their interactions with the people they meet. What is common to all their stories is an openness to experience, an eagerness to transcend the familiar self. Sometimes there's hurt, too, because real travel, like real life, is not covered with a warranty. These wonderful myriad voices remind us that getting away is sometimes the real route home.

—Sandra Scofield, author of
Gringa and *Occasions of Sin: A Memoir*

Nearly two dozen American women wander into the vast world-next-door that is our neighbor to the south. With equal measures of curiosity and courage, they journey to sunny resorts, grim penitentiaries, and time-challenged villages. Like them, you will be enchanted and amazed.

—Héctor Tobar, author of *Translation Nation: Defining a New American Identity in the Spanish-Speaking United States*

With open minds and hearts, these writers engage Mexico in all its sensual, spiritual, confounding glory and emerge transformed.

—Gina Hyams, author of *In a Mexican Garden*

This wide-ranging collection of gringa experiences in Mexico shines a light upon, and becomes a part of, one of the most charged cultural conversations on earth: that between North Americans and their southern neighbors.

—Tony Cohan, author of *On Mexican Time* and *Mexican Days*

For *France, A Love Story*

This is a very readable collection . . . Tales are alternately loving, witty, nostalgic, and yes, occasionally swooning.

—*San Francisco Chronicle*

In this beautiful collection, women share their experiences firsthand, reflecting on the ways France's unique culture has enriched and enchanted their lives.

—*France Today*

The heart of this book is in the maturity of its voices of experience.

—*Boston Globe*

This book is an evocative gathering of short pieces from twenty-five female writers . . . This is a collection that will be appreciated by the Francophiles among us.

—*Toronto Globe and Mail*

For *Greece, A Love Story*

Nineteen brave women pursue a vanishing Greece, bridging chasms of language and culture with their bodies and their tears. This book should be read not only by travelers aspiring to a mythic, well-explored landscape but also by the Greek fishermen into whose unfathomable brown eyes so many alien women have poured so much hope.

—Bradley Kiesling, author of *Diplomacy Lessons: Realism for an Unloved Superpower*

A shockingly beautiful collection. Ancient mythology informs these modern journeys, making them as enchanting as they are intimately real.

—Ariel Gore, author of
Atlas of the Human Heart and
The Traveling Death and Resurrection Show

For *Tango, an Argentine Love Story*

Tango is a remarkable addition to contemporary dharma literature. It reads like a thriller, a romance, and above all it shows the redemptive potential of a sincere spiritual practice.

—Sylvia Boorstein, PhD, author of
Happiness is an Inside Job

The transformative power of the tango embrace beautifully captured. Bravo!

—Marina Palmer, author of *Kiss & Tango*

Camille Cusumano has lived out many a mid-life woman's fantasy: packing her bags, slit skirts, and tango shoes and spending a year in Argentina. The result is a memoir that is like the dance itself: smooth, absorbing, and erotically charged.

—Laura Fraser, author of *An Italian Affair*

The author "recounts her journey toward self-awareness set in the context of an extraordinary year spent in Buenos Aires. According to Cusumano, tango—like yoga and Zen, which she also practices— is a way of life, and her keen and colorful observations of everything from the *milongas* (tango dance halls) and her dance wardrobe to the people she met and danced with to the neighborhoods she lived in and the foods she ate create a thoughtful account redolent with the sights, sounds, and tastes of her own tango experience. Cusumano's book is recommended for public library collections serving dancers, armchair travelers, and literary-essay fans.

—Carolyn M. Mulac, Chicago P.L. *School Library Journal*

In her memoir, the author's accounts of passionate, sweaty tango dances are reinterpreted through her explanation of Zen. In this sense the reader comes to understand how tango, as Cusumano puts it, is not a "vice" but a "virtue," as it becomes a way to fall in love with Argentina."

—*The Argentimes*

"If you've ever loved and lost, *Tango: An Argentine Love Story* will ring true. After a failed relationship, the author heads to Argentina--and finds mouthwatering cuisine, welcoming people, and a passion for dance. Though it may take two to tango, the lesson here is how to live happily on your own."

— *Shape Magazine*

For *Quantum Tango*

In this Zen koan of a novella, Camille Cusumano explores the ineffable, the Tango Moment. Cusumano uses her words and phrases with the flamboyant precision of the accomplished tanguera she is, and just as the quest for the sublime Tango Moment keeps us returning again and again to the dance floor, you will want to read this enchanting book again and again.

—Jamie Rose, author of *Shut Up and Dance!*
The Joy of Letting Go of the Lead

WILDERNESS BEGINS AT HOME

Travels With My Big Sicilian Family

Camille Cusumano

Dedicated to Mom, Dad, and their One called

JimmyTerryChuckSalCamilleGraceTommyLisaTinaDonna

Centanni Publications
Slow-cooked words for hungry minds
www.centannipublications.com
San Francisco, California

WILDERNESS BEGINS AT HOME

Travels with my big Sicilian family

Camille Cusumano

About the author

Camille Cusumano is the author of *Tango, an Argentine Love Story* (Seal Press, 2008), memoir of a woman who loved, lost, got mad, and decided to dance. She has written for numerous publications, including *National Geographic Traveler*, *Islands*, *Country Living*, the *San Francisco Chronicle*, *Los*  *Angeles Times*, *Christian Science Monitor*, the *New York Times*, and the *Washington Post*. She is the author of several cookbooks and one novel, *The Last Cannoli* (Legas) and the editor of the literary travel anthologies on France, Italy, Mexico, and Greece. She was a senior staff editor at *VIA Magazine* in San Francisco, where she covered travel around the world. In October, 2013, she presented a TEDx Talk in Manhattan's Lower Eastside on Tango as hero's journey.

Centanni Publications
www.centannipublications.com
San Francisco, California

Wilderness Begins at Home
Copyright © 2015 by Camille Cusumano
Printed in the United States of America
Centanni Publications, San Francisco, California

The author gratefully acknowledges that all or part of some of the stories in this collection appeared in *VIA Magazine*, *Los Angeles Times*, and *Islands Magazine*, or in anthologies by Seal Press, publishers of books by and for women.

Sky Pilot lyrics: Eric Burdon, Vic Briggs, John Weider, Barry Jenkins, Danny McCulloch; Eric Burdon and the Animals, February 1968.

All rights reserved. No part of this book may be reproduced or transmitted in any form or by any means, electronic or mechanical, including photocopy, recording, or any information storage and retrieval system now known or to be invented, without the express permission in writing from the publisher or author, except by a reviewer who wishes to quote brief passages in connection with a review written for inclusion in a magazine, newspaper, or broadcast.

FIRST EDITION

ISBN-13: 978-0997049831
ISBN-10: 0997049839

Book cover design: Ingalls Design, ingallsdesign.com
Author photo: Daniel J. Taaffe
Interior design: Valentina Dante

Requests for permission to reprint material:
Centanni Publications
ocaramia2000@gmail.com
(415) 425-6515
www.centannipublications.com
www.camillecusumano.com

TABLE OF CONTENTS

11

Introduction

It was not the first time my father had blood in his eye. He calmly removed the sabre and the small pistol from their brackets over the hearth in the den. Both items had been gifts from my brother, Salvatore, an Air Force Academy graduate and pilot during the Vietnam War. The mementoes appealed to our father, a boastful veteran of World War II who never left his hawkish military days behind.

It might have taken ten minutes for Dad to walk down Main Street and find the blasted plumber in this blasted rural Ringtown, Pennsylvania, the ham 'n' egger who had double-crossed him. My parents, "open-door" Italians, never really adapted to the more reserved Pennsylvania Dutch culture in which they lived during the 1970s, raising the four youngest of their ten children. Now all the disappointment and hurt boiled up in one lousy incident.

Oliver (a pseudonym) had done work on a septic system and my father had paid with a $500 check. Ollie told my father that he had put the check that Dad had given him in his work pants, his wife washed them, so he needed a new check. Dad readily made out a second payment but not before locking eyes with Oliver, a known gambler, and saying, "Don't mess with me." Oliver proceeded to cash both checks. He didn't think my father would notice—perhaps because in those days, Dad's early retirement and sudden idleness led to his heaviest drinking yet. Oliver was wrong.

Happy or sad, my father never had trouble making his presence known. He found Oliver doing work up the street. He easily got Oliver's attention. He put the gun to Ollie's head and the knife to his stomach and asked, "Which end do you want it first?" The townsmen nearby who intercepted my father's would-be crime of passion (passion, despite his warrior serene exterior) convinced him, not without some rigorous coaxing, that Ollie was not worth the trouble that killing or harming the feckless fellow would entail.

This story, now firmly ensconced in our pantheon of family mythology, is perhaps the most hair-raising of those my siblings and I witnessed over the years. There's the car chase after teen boys, Dad swinging his police baton, because the boys had flirted with my sister and me, aged fourteen and fifteen. Thankfully, the bewildered boys got away. And the time Dad threatened the persistent Jehovah Witness canvasser that he would cut his throat ear to ear and call it self defense if he didn't depart our home PDQ. There are many eye-rolling brinkmanship stories about our father who art heaven—going on twelve years now.

I give you a mere cursory glimpse of such anecdotes about my father to offer an inkling of where my nine siblings and I came from. And what my obedient mother quietly witnessed and endured. This book is not about that wild father per se, although he will invariably make cameo appearances in these stories.

I believe that art has given us enough representatives of Dad's archetype. In varying degrees, my father echoes the drunken fathers-of-ten in true-story movies, *My Left Foot* and *The Prizewinner of Defiance Ohio*, and the father in *The Great Santini* who runs his family like a boot camp. He might have reminded me of the father in Pat Conroy's *The Prince of Tides* except my father was never mean for the sake of meanness. He was mean for other reasons, including his own unexamined demons and rigid adherence to excessively tough love.

Rather, this book is a collection of stories written over nearly twenty years, some of them published in shorter versions in magazines or newspapers. I fill you in on the family backstory where fitting.

The sort of big family in which I was bred, despite its *wildness,* is becoming a relic of the past. Not just because the size—ten kids + two parents—is prohibitive and undesirable for most in the developed world. But the nuclear-family model that influenced the high and low points of my upbringing is for practical, economic, and cultural reasons fading. In an article in the *London Review of Books* (September 24, 2015), James Meek noted "The nuclear family has become the quantum family, its particles entangled over vast stretches of space. And vast stretches of time." Let's note that quantum particles often have strong attractive charges that space and time cannot disentangle.

I have often been asked what it was like growing up in a big Sicilian (American) family. The closest I have ever come to honestly answering that question was the novel, *The Last Cannoli* (Legas, 2000). It was easier to answer with a fictional approach, which was, of course, only a thin veil over the truth (plus some half truths and some truths-and-a-half). There were good times and bad times and I remember them all. But I preferred to focus on the good times in that "faux memoir" and if I gave short shrift to the bad, I make no apologies. I do not ignore the difficult facts, including my father's alcoholism and meanness. But we have a rare, if disappearing, strength in our big family ties.

Twelve of us, two parents and ten kids *rhythm*ically spaced about two years apart, grew up together in a tiny home in New Jersey. Given the distance that our various walks in life has put between us, sharing travels is the way we get together, the way we reunite. These stories span 1991 to 2015. They take place in our adult years, when we have grown, entered the marketplace, and flourished.

Many of these stories bring to light my connections to wilderness, which started late in life, unlike my family, which started very early in life. What came to the fore as I wrote many of these stories was how the wilderness is often an escape *from* something; for me it has proved an escape *into*— the past, the forces that shaped me, most notably my large family, the crowded household, and the natural forces I longed for, and which my childhood was short on.

As you will see, a number of these travel stories take place in the backcountry wilderness. The practice of the wild, the practice of walking, of breathing and observing, converge at my practice of writing. My stories are not so much about *the edges between human activity and the natural world* (a phrase I read somewhere and cannot find its original author) as the threads that bind these. I contemplate my experience as family myth (like *Romulus and Remus*, say) and how I've progressed from the wilds of nurture to the etiquette of nature. My parents, stewards of my earliest habitat, gave me my first hard lessons in *leaving no trace*.

The continuum from quotidian life to sojourns in the wilderness is eminently more valuable to me than the compartmentalizing of the two. My avid reading of California poet, Gary Snyder, has led me to see wilderness this way, as the sacred mirror of what lurks within ourselves.

Thus, what I mean to sum up is that my travel stories, whether in the literal backcountry wilds or in the front country urban wilds, graft family mythology onto these trips with varying mixtures of irony, humor, joy, sadness. My travels with my five sisters, who are as I describe, "a wilderness unto themselves," have a different, yet wildly native, flavor than those with my brothers.

Wilderness Begins at Home, the title story, recounts how a grueling weeklong backpack trip to Mount Whitney will be the last walk in the woods for one in our party of two families (mine and my partner's), but some of us will come back more deeply rooted in the earth. In *Saving Grace*, I introduce a sister from Union City, New Jersey, to western snowmelt in the Trinity Alps, confront a swarm of bats, as we rediscover our relationship, which was put on pause years before in New Jersey. And there's the time I coaxed even my not-so-active family members to climb a mountain to a rustic inn for an unforgettable family reunion.

Time to meet the clan. Whether your preference is for travel amid earthy wilds or in the civilized front country, I hope you enjoy travels with my big Sicilian family.

I won't ask you to keep our names straight.

1

La Familia,
Stanno Tutti Bene in Sicilia, 2006

A family reunion in the old country—it had such a nice ring to it. But when I read my brother Tom's email suggesting our clan meet in Sicily come summer, I had misgivings. He doesn't remember what it was like, I thought, the 12 of us—10 siblings and two parents— under one small roof, sharing one-and-a-half bathrooms all those years ago.

These days, a family gathering means more than 50 people when you include Mom, spouses, and 39 kids and grandkids. And then there would be a few dozen relatives on the other side of the Atlantic, three generations of our late father's first cousins. That's a lot of pressure on the plumbing, not to mention the nerves.

I love my family to no end. We are your classic tight knit big family. Our affectionate (and sometimes querulous) emails stream over the Internet. Birth, christening, marriage, and occasionally an elder's passing on are annual mandates for our inimitable brand of Sicilian conviviality.

Yet, if you look at the distance we've put between each other since leaving that overcrowded nest—our homes spread from New Jersey to California, from Prague to Timor, and down to Buenos Aires—you might conclude as I did that we required a lot of space to vacation together.

I knew that many "normal" families happily cruised together on city-size ships. But, I didn't think that even a whole island was big enough for the likes of our mercurial bunch.

OK, so I was wrong this once.

It turned out to be one of the best family vacations since our parents stuffed ten of us, crates of food, and beach paraphernalia into a station wagon for a few days at (poor) Uncle Pasquale's beach house at the Jersey shore.

In fact, there was a fairytale aspect from the moment I arrived in Cefalú, on Sicily's northern coast. The Mediterranean Sea and a sheer craggy rampart of the Madonie Mountains picturesquely frame the popular resort, an hour's drive from Palermo. Brightly painted wooden fishing boats park on sand or rock beaches where warm and gentle glass-blue waves lap the shore.

The family home for the next week was a palace. The Palazzo Maria, a far cry from the box we had grown up in, was a restored medieval building, with a restaurant and enoteca (wine shop) on its ground floor. Bordering the Piazza Duomo, our palace rose five floors catty-corner to the imposing 12th-century basilica, or Duomo, with its two steeples, abbey, and cloister built under the reign of Roger II.

Tom, who undertook the yeoman's task of booking our lodgings and planning the week's events—which would include festivities with the Sicilian branch several days after our arrival—did well in choosing Cefalú as a base. It offers a crowd-pleasing mix of beauty, outdoor activities, shopping, art galleries, cultural sights, and, of course, plenty of restaurants.

Cefalú comes from the Greek word (*Kephaloidion*) for head—and it's instantly apparent why this name was bestowed on the area. The "heady" Rocca, a massively bulging promontory, 270 meters high, dominates the village. A crenellated wall and other ancient ruins crown its summit. If you don't mind a stair-master-from-hell workout, you can hike to breathtaking (literally and figuratively) views and ruins.

Another plus was that from Cefalú one can easily take day-long or overnight excursions by car to any of Sicily's important sites. One day, a group of us drove to Agrigento to walk the impressive Valley of the Temples. Within easy drives on Sicily's well-maintained auto-routes are Erice with its lofty perch and mystical pre-Greek vestiges; Taormina, the aptly-called "aristocratic jewel" above the Ionian Sea; Siracusa with its abundance of ancient sites and archeological treasures; and Selinunte and Segesta where there are also Greek temples and ruins. A hydrofoil offered daily departures from Cefalú's harbor to the Aeolian Islands. But for me, having traveled Sicily often over the past thirty years, la dolce vita under my nose and spending time with family was enough.

The only drawback was that not everyone could make the voyage. My oldest brother Jim's wife became pregnant and would deliver at the time of the trip; my youngest sister, Donna, couldn't leave her United Nations post in

East Timor, due to outbursts of civil unrest there (the country fought a brutal civil war to break away from Indonesia); and poor Mom, 84, fell and broke her hip and was still in rehab come her departure date.

However, 32 of us made a good show. Over several days in late June, we arrived to storm the palace and its six spacious, antique-furnished apartments. Each sported a plaque on its door with its name—Ruggero, Turiddu, Costanza, Guglielmo, Federico, and Joanna—and all were decorated in a rich palette of primary colors. A few families spilled over into apartments a five-minute walk from there, but the palazzo with its splendid rooftop terrace would be the nightly gathering area. We'd run in and out of each other's flats to visit and see who had the best-stocked pantry and fridge.

Just like the old days, I shared my quarters, the airy royal-blue interior of Turiddu, with two sisters, Tina and Grace. We loved sitting on our little third-floor balcony with its views to sunset over the sea and the Aeolians or watching the bustle below in the cobbled square with its fringe of cafes and boutiques.

We could see who among our group was exercising his or her blood-right to *far niente* (do nothing) in the cafes whose espresso machines we kept hissing and whose stock of custard-filled brioches and cannoli we seriously depleted.

From the piazza, each day, by and by, a clutch of us would make the five-minute stroll to the main beach down narrow streets, sometimes clogged with cars and small fruit-delivery trucks. On the way, we'd pass the Museo Mandralisca, which holds archeological artifacts, such as Greek and Arab vases, old coins, and paintings, including the Renaissance Portrait of a Man by Antonello da Messina. Shops overflowing with lovely hand-painted ceramic wares, much of them from nearby San Stefano di Camestre and Caltanisetta, would stall us in our tracks.

We'd stop to marvel at the waters still running into basins under a pink stone arch in the *lavatoio medievale*, a former village laundro-mat that dates from the Middle Ages. We walked through another venerable Arab archway, called the Porta Pescara, and, *ecco*, there was the broad scallop of sandy beach plastered with wall-to-wall towels. In summer, Cefalú can get packed with sunbathers, but none of us minded them, especially the hand-gesticulating crowds, who recalled the Italian ghetto of our youth in New Jersey.

Occasionally, I took refuge in the relative solitude of a beach at the edge of town past the lighthouse and Torre Calura, a rocky tower ruin. To get there I had to walk a brisk fifteen minutes, hugging the coast, through the Porta Giudecca, the historic Jewish neighborhood (which disappointed my Jewish brother-in-law, Dan, for its lack of an interpretive plaque); past the boat harbor; and little cottages fronted with bougainvillea, lanterna, and oleander. After a libation on the cliff-top terrace of the Hotel Calura, I'd climb down the staircase about 200 feet to the secluded beach and swim out to a rock with snorkelers.

Early or late in the day, when the sun was not so intense, some of us would make the invigorating climb up the Rocca, following the signs and arrows up steep alleys or stone staircases, then walking the dirt trail until we were atop the sheer precipice. Amid stone pines we looked vertiginously down on the Duomo and out to sea for miles. It was absolutely stunning. There were many relics to visit on the way up, including ninth-century castle ruins, a couple of small churches, ancient cisterns, the fortress wall that belted the Rocca's precipitous border, and my favorite, a small pre-Christian Temple to Diana where I would spend some contemplative time.

One afternoon, my brother, Sal, and I walked along the rocky seacoast where young bronzed men with well-defined muscles were spear fishing for octopus (pulpo). They showed us how they stored the ghostly white fish, which appeared on many village menus, in a tide pool with seaweed. As Sal and I slid off the rock into the clear water to cool off, I said, "I hope they don't mistake our legs for octopus tentacles."

We laughed and bobbed in the salty sea and as we soaked in the perfection of the moment—the sun's warmth in a cloudless blue sky, the Rocca facing us like a forbidding monolith onshore—we decided we would cook the family meal that night. This was a harmonious change from our standard political debates.

That night we added our own sizzling garlic to the smells that wafted out from the nearby restaurants. The sausage and rigatoni we cooked up for our masses was just one of our memorable meals that brought us together on the palace roof. After a long, hard day of sun, sand, and sea, we'd take siestas, and showers, then sip aperitifs on the square. Dinner, with respect for local custom, was never before 9 p.m. We'd all contribute goods gathered from the many town purveyors.

A spread might include marinated sardines, tangy caponata, an array of sharp and creamy cheeses, crusty breads, fresh peaches and figs, oil-cured olives, prosciutto, pepperoni, sun dried tomatoes, pesto dip, bitter greens, local olive oil, and arancini (deep-fried rice balls stuffed with meat, cheese, and veggies).

One night, my sister, Terry, made cucuzza, a tomato-rich dish packed with memories of our grandmother who grew the long crooked green squash in her garden in Elizabeth, New Jersey. Nostalgia came in many bites—from the eggplant appetizer, biscotti, and Torrone nougat candy to the many bottles of red wine, especially the popular Cusumano label (which we pretend is our relative).

Strains of Mob Hits, The Big Night soundtrack, and Pavarotti sounded from Tom's iPod as the lemoncello, Fra Angelica, and Sambuca flowed into glasses after dinner. We shot digital photos against the stunningly spotlighted Rocca and occasionally danced and sang with the little kids. We told the same old family stories but with new twists and turns, over and over, until 4 a.m.

One afternoon, Chuck's wife, Cheri, asked a local store owner where she could find good cheese. Good cheese, she enunciated slowly to help him understand her English. Ah, *si,* he replied, as he proceeded to gesture vigorously for her to go straight down the main drag, *uno, due, tre* blocks and *ecco,* there on the left gooood cheeeese." Cheri followed the directions carefully only to arrive at a corner with not a one cheese shop in sight, but a shoe store selling Gucci shoes. We laughed about that homonymous snag for a long time.

Although there were plenty of restaurants, our best meals were our own up on the roof. Several of us had had a few disappointments in the local eateries—no doubt the result of too many tourists in town. However, two places pleased us. We enjoyed the seafood and pasta dishes at Ostaria di duomo and Il Saraceno, both of which seemed capable of dealing with our unwieldy crowd.

Then came time for the Big Moment—the raison d'etre of our trip—the reunion with the cousins in the two villages, San Giovanni-Gemini and Cammarata, where our respective maternal and paternal grandparents were born. Only a handful of us had ever met the Sicilian branch. They, occupying the land of our bloodline since time immemorial, had never set foot on American soil. Only one in their group spoke some English, while only about four of us spoke some Italian.

A bus transported nearly three dozen of us to the neighboring villages, about two hours south of Cefalu. Many of us sat silently gazing out at the passing landscape, harsh and rugged, yet in places irrigated to a quilt-work of lushness to grow food. Tom pointed out Monte Cammarata, the highest point, over 5,000 feet, in southern Sicily.

Watching the bones of rock pierce through a velvet-green mantled peak, some of us thought sadly how our father should have been here for this historic meeting. He had seen Sicily only once, late in his life. But he drilled us as kids about how the island was a crossroads for every tribe of people—the Phoenicians, Greeks, Romans, and the Serbs, Goths, Vandals, Saracens, Arabs, Normans, Byzantines, and Spanish. When he was feeling especially proud of his heritage, he had told us we were not Italian, but Sicilian. He had many pithy sayings, including his favorite, *Salsiccia his own* (a word-play on To each-a his own)

The bus, too long and wide to travel the village-proper streets, deposited us in a square of San Giovanni. Our cousin, Rena Tuzzolino, and her husband Enzo Maggio met us and after a hundred hugs and kisses took place began touring us on foot through the village, which I first saw some 30 years ago. It had not changed much since then and as always its Middle-Age past was still in strong evidence in many edifices.

Thirty-two of us, ranging in age from eight months to sixty-one, followed Rena and Enzo up and down narrow, winding cobbled streets. Taller than the average Sicilian and dressed like foreigners, with our Teva and Birkenstock sandals, we were a curiosity. Although my siblings and I are no less Sicilian, blood-wise, than our father's cousins, our next two generations are a classic American stew seasoned with Irish, English, Norwegian,

Ukraine, Russian, Philippine, Chinese, and African American blood. Old villagers came out of their dark doorways to peek at us and greet us with friendly nods, smiles, or handshakes.

Ducking under many sturdy archways erected during Arab rule, we visited the old Norman Church, the castle ruins, and stopped by a nondescript gray stone house. We peered in at its ground floor where animals were once kept. This was where our grandfather was born in 1887. In 1903, he set sail on the Palatia from Hamburg, Germany, for America, coming through Ellis Island. He died at age fifty-one in 1938 and never met any of his grandchildren.

Across the way, lived Nicolo Tuzzolino, our Dad's Sicilian counterpart. The reigning patriarch and his wife, Concetta, dwell on the top floor of the four-story marble and concrete home that also houses their four children and seven grandchildren. The home is built into a steep hillside and many times I have savored, from its terrace, vistas of the alternately straw-brown or farm-green land. On clear days, I've seen all the way to smoking Mount Etna.

I watched seventy-nine-year-old Nicolo's swarthy face, framed by wine-dark hair, light up as he received us. In the past, when some of us have shown up at his home, he has burst in tears of joy. But when my father came in 1998, he was paranoid briefly that it was to reclaim the land my grandfather left behind.

Paces away from Nicolo's home, Rena and Enzo led our straggling procession to the town hall, where the mayor, Vito Mangiapane (who shares a surname with our maternal great grandmother) met us and gave each of us a signed book on the history of Cammarata. He told us he was honored that we made the long trip back to his little mountain village of 6,500 inhabitants. He pointed to the town's age-old emblem—a woman nursing a serpent on either of her breasts. It was designed by a Spanish count to represent how the Cammaratesi welcomed foreigners. "Nourish others and let yourself go hungry," Rena translated the symbolism, explaining how the people here had always welcomed strangers.

This revelation of such extreme generosity hit a nerve as we all remembered how anyone—friend or stranger—who appeared on our doorstep at meal time was invited to sit and eat. I recalled a letter from my father, years into his empty nest, in which he said he was in the process of "adopting 10 more kids (from around the world), one for each of you guys," spreading his postal-worker pension thinner than we could imagine.

That evening in nearby Casteltermini more than fifty of us sat down together to break bread—and twirl pasta—in the Lupo Nero, the restaurant in the agriturismo Parco Sette Lune, a 300-acre reserve with horses, donkeys, skeet shooting, and hunting. Tom, who had just begun discovering Sicily in 2000 and meeting with the warmth and hospitality of our Sicilian kin, had gone all out and even had commemorative T-shirts made for every one of us. They featured an insignia with our names and the date with the bright red and gold, Trinacria, the ancient three-legged symbol of the tri-cornered island. Best of all, each of us received a seven-foot-wide family tree dating back to 1834 that Tom, Rena, and Enzo had assembled.

As we all sat and marveled how Tom's planning of this impossibly successful trip led to this moment, he stood and gave a twenty-minute *brindisi,* or toast. Tom spoke the English and his fluent Italian-speaker daughter, Christina, (who dates home-grown Sicilian men), repeated all in Italian.

Punch drunk on wine, food, toasts, and the hyper-smiling and gesturing one does to reach across a gap of language, time, and place, we all stayed up late, well past exhaustion.

Back in Cefalú we still had a whole weekend to recover. Each day, we slowly collected in an al fresco café and discussed for hours where the day might go. The church bells might remind us there was a thing called time. We avoided the heated, nerve-jangling political debates our family often engages in. Topics of conversation were nothing more controversial than whether to have a second espresso, where to shop—for *gooood* cheese or Guccis—, or who did nephew Michael's new, fat baby, Olivia, who was born in Italy, look like.

It was as if after years of having gone out into the world to slay our respective dragons, we were able to finally *far niente*—do nothing but savor *la dolce vita.* In this sense, this trip was a coming home of the most memorable sort. Oh, and last I heard, Palazzo Maria has had no plumbing problems.

Guidelines that made our family reunion abroad successful:

1. We had, Tom, one person willing to take charge of the big planning—finding a suitable place, lodgings, time frame.

2. Tom used our family email list to check in regularly on who was on board with the idea. Since we spread from Prague to California, the Internet was indispensable for us.

3. He began to plan the trip and its time frame about eight months ahead of time. Because we have teachers in our family, we were not able to choose off-season times, which would have been cheaper.

4. We had the benefit of Tom's having been to Cefalu and seen the lodgings. But still for our large group he needed to work with someone abroad.

5. Each individual or families were responsible for their own airline arrangements, but we shared tips on possible airfare bargains.

6. When planning this far out, it's important to check on lodging cancellation policies.

7. And trip insurance would have saved my brother, Jim, the loss of a lot of money on our mother's first class airfare. Mom fell and broke her hip and was still in rehab come departure time.

8. If people had gripes with their lodgings (invariably they do) once they arrived, it was their responsibility to work it out with Massimo, our Sicilian contact, not Tom, who had done his best to meet requirements.

9. Never discuss politics on a family vacation. We were golden here.

10. Eat, drink, and recall the good times with gusto.

2

Always a Father,
Sometimes a God, 1998

We would be nothing but for our blood. It's a debatable point, but one on which my father and I agree. That we share any hardwiring—let alone blood—always gives me pause. My father is a man who is given to remorseless outbursts of misogyny. He yells at the TV's female announcers to "go home and have babies." He makes no bones about his belief that with women in the workplace the world is in a downward spiral.

"I'm sorry, I can't change the way I feel," is his summary dismissal of any argument. Except for a rare lapse in restraint, I no longer argue with him.

I was preparing for my third trip to Sicily from which my blood flows, on both maternal and paternal sides, when my oldest brother, Jim, said, "Take Dad and Mom."

It was a sound request. My father could recite Sicilian history, chapter and verse, yet neither he nor my mother had set foot on the birth soil of their parents. He needed to see Sicily before he died, but hadn't I become a world traveler in part to escape my father and his constricting views? As I pondered the prospect of being abroad with my father, novelty changed to prospect. Then, Jim, known affectionately as Numero Uno, added resolutely, "Spare no expense, I'll pay." Done deal.

It's one thing to visit a Greek temple. It's another to think that maybe one of your very own ancestors built that spectacular rise of well-proportioned stone. Fanciful as it is, that's the thought that has often flashed through my mind during my trips to Sicily. Unbeknownst to Americans, Sicily has more temples than Greece, having been part of the Roman, Greek and Byzantine empires. Ask a Sicilian about this, however, and you will learn that the great mathematician Archimedes was born in Siracusa. Ask my father and you will hear that Dante was enchanted by the polyglot Sicilian language and that God planted the Garden of Eden there.

My father's relentless boasting of Sicily's undervalued greatness inspired my first trip to the island in 1976. Panicky about meeting my father's cousins, I made a pilgrimage of sorts to the Valley of the Temples in Agrigento where four of these monuments stand in a harmonious line on a ridge overlooking the Mediterranean. I had no idea how to invoke the support of the temples' gods—Castor and Pollux, the patrons of sailors, the mighty Hercules, and the moody Hera, but I left feeling fortified.

More than twenty years later, I was there again, with Dad and Mom in tow. We found the same pink and gold maritime light suffusing the shrines where divine auguries transpired twenty-five centuries before. The irony that the cult of the Great Mother was responsible for many of these stone relics may have escaped my father, but it gave me silent pleasure.

33

A softer patriarch at age 78, my father sat on a ledge in the scant shade of an acacia tree and said his rosary. He needed to rest the weak heart and lungs that lay behind a serpentlike scar down his chest. Twice he has had his rib cage cracked open, like a crab, so doctors could reposition vessels and tubes to keep his heart pumping properly. During one episode, his heart stopped beating for a few minutes. ("He's got more bypasses than L.A. has freeways," my siblings and I have joked.) He has come back from the brink more than once, with part of him inexorably tough as nails.

Leaving him to pray, my mother and I slowly climbed the ridge to pay homage to the gods and goddesses of our ancestors. I thought briefly how Mom and I fit the Greek myth of Demeter and Persephone. In a way I was like the latter, hustled, not to Hades, but to another "underworld" in my Mother's eyes—living unconventionally and embracing libertine ways. I would have loved a mother who had the ferocious persona of Ms. D. But instead of blowing her frosty breath on the earth like Demeter, my mother simply prays the rosary for me—and many others.

As she and I rested in the long shadow of the 34 fluted columns of the Temple of Concordia, I thought about my father. Weak and vulnerable and in need of my navigating strength, both physical and mental, he was once as invincible and almighty as any Greek god.

When I was growing up, the fifth of his ten kids, our family of twelve sat down to supper together every evening. The routine was as familiar to each of us as church liturgy. My mother, by Dad's decree, served us kids first, him last, then she sat at his right side. We remained silent until we had bowed our heads as one to say grace. At the height of the Cold War, we tacked on a prayer for peace to the Blessed Virgin Mary, the *Memorare*. No one conversed until our father, who sat at the head of the rectangular Formica table, gave the word and sometimes he didn't. As we ate every morsel of food on our plates, Dad's forbidding dark eyes glanced around to make sure each one was eating a hunk of bread, the better to fill so many bellies. No one dared think of leaving the table until we were all done and then only with express permission: "Dad, may I please be excused?" Sometimes he said no.

Failing to show up for this sacrosanct meal without prior excuse or even arriving a few minutes late could mean a whipping with his belt (sons and daughters both). He was unswervingly strict and adherent to corporal punishment.

Somewhere along the line, having garnered romantic notions of the Mafia, I wondered why a tough guy like my father had not been a Man of Honor. I asked him and he said "They asked me to drive a truck during Prohibition but I said no." He said "they" also "asked" his father to let them store booze in their cellar. My grandfather said don't tell me what it is—it's flour, right? My father never bad mouthed the Mafia and was more likely to get riled over media slurs on Italians and join force with those in New Jersey who believed John Rigghi, of the "Elizabeth Crew" got a bum rap due to his nationality.

That tyrant is all but gone, I thought, as I drove my parents around the isle of our forebears, remembering the good ties that bound us, too, like our shared reverence for a fine repast. We strolled Palermo's *Vucciria* market purchasing olives, sesame seeded bread, asiago, fresh figs, and tomatoes for a picnic lunch. My father and I were entranced by the city's ancient sites—the Cathedral, the Royal Palace with its Palatine Chapel, and Monreale with its glittering mosaics. My mother hung back, distracted or bored, but he and I absorbed the awesome message of the architecture—an Arab arch or Moorish dome here, a Norman steeple or Roman façade there. The unusual mix bespeaks centuries of cultural one-upmanship. I wonder to myself, how much historical grief over all the trampling infused our own blood?

Driving to Taormina, the aristocratic jewel over the Ionian Sea, my mother sat quietly in the backseat, a place she has known intimately in deference to my father for nearly sixty years of marriage. We stopped often in tiny villages to appease my father's restroom needs. At each stop, he found some friendly stranger happy to listen to him recall his first tongue. *"Mi chiamo Calogero, no parlo Italiano, parlo Sicilian' antica."* (My name is Calogero—his baptismal name, changed by his first school teacher to Charles—I don't speak Italian, I speak old Sicilian.) Leaning on his cane, waxing proud on his heritage, my father fit right in with his audience of aging, bent villagers.

Through the sun-drenched countryside we traveled, my father frequently breaking into songs, some of which he had made up decades ago (including *We are the Cusumanos*, sung to the tune of *Macnamara's Band*). In his younger days, his moods could turn on a dime. His dark ones were hellish, but when they were good, all was right with the world. Then he would express his love for us kids and my mother, often with hyperbole—he "loved us more than life itself." He told the little kids funny stories ("the world will end when there are no more Popsicle sticks.") and led us through sing-alongs (*Oh Marie!* and *Bill Grogan's Goat* were some of his favorites). He wrote love songs to my mother after he had tested her good nature by making difficult demands—usually some sort of "gag order"—*Don't question my authority, you are my wife, destined to love, honor, and obey me.*

In Taormina, his charismatic side was fully engaged. As my mother perused the art in a gallery, he and the artist, Giolini, entertained patrons with a Sicilian folksong, *Quel Mazzolin dei fiori*. At the ancient Greek Theater, he admonished a guard, "Stop whistling and sing through your mouth!" They broke into *Faniculi, fanicula*. His antics continued through dinner.

The waiters all but kissed the ground he stood on and addressed him as Padrino, as he bragged of his ten kids and thirty three grand- and great-grandkids. When he pretended that the perfectly cooked veal parmigiana was only so-so, the headwaiter said, "I will kill the cook."

37

On the other hand, the drivers, especially those in Palermo who have zero tolerance for floundering tourists, awakened a shadow of my father's former hair-trigger road rage. As I drove, he blurted out, "G'head, you ham 'n egger, you couldn't give us break . . . Ah, cryin' out loud, blow your horn out the other end. . . that's right, cut in front like the *gavun'* you are. . ."

I let him chatter away, perhaps still harboring the little girl who feared him. The first eighteen years of my life I was my father's obedient daughter, before I went on to flout his flags to God, country, and family: I didn't marry or bear children, practiced Zen Buddhism and forsook Catholicism, and demonstrated against wars—all of which he believes are right and just. But earth has no wrath or fury like my father's. So I prefer to sit on my convictions than to express them and excite his righteous indignation, which can whither me no less today than it did when I was an adolescent. "In my home, everyone is entitled to my opinion," reads a sign—only half in jest—over a transom in my father's house.

Between 13th-century stone walls in Cammarata, my paternal grandfather's village, came a defining moment. I was tense negotiating a narrow cobblestone alley built in the Middle Ages for hoofed beasts, which now passed as a road for motor vehicles. The ocher-colored feudal dwellings closed in, not even inches from either side of the shiny purple rented Opal. Suddenly, a loud clap resounded in the car—the side-view mirror banged shut as I got too close to the wall. My father had been trying to guide me on his side but I preferred my own animal instinct. I muttered the F word under my breath, a word I hadn't ever used in his presence. He sensed my disapproval. "I was just trying to help," he said wistfully.

There, to the sound of metal scraping stone, I realized that he feared me more than I feared him. I saw that I was, in his eyes, an adult, not a withering adolescent. I should have known this—after all, hadn't he placed implicit trust in me by being my charge on this trip? And there have been precious moments in our past, when my father, in stunning recognition of who I have become, discussed heart to heart with me subjects like Thomas Merton and mysticism or how the breath comes and goes in meditation. Although it wasn't the first time he had perceived me as an adult, it was first time I fully absorbed the course of our role reversal. It is liberating and excruciating when old familial roles, even those as calcified as a limestone wall, crumble.

In that instant, I felt sorry for him. Not for the first time. I had felt sorrow that both his father and his mother died minutes before he reached their deathbeds; that he had been injured in World War II and sent home with a bad back for life. That he had come stateside from war on a Friday and showed up for work on a Monday, having no transition period to civilian life. He was edgy after returning and given to slapping his one-and-a-half-year old son, born in his absence, for slamming doors. He was haunted for years by the gore of war in the South Pacific, of which he spoke freely, especially during his drinking career. After taking an early retirement for the back injury, he became in mid-life a full-fledged alcoholic and only went into recovery at age 58 after several stunning spectacles.

Exiting from the tight 13th-century walls onto an open piazza, we faced the modern four-story home of my father's first cousin, Nicola Tuzzolino. Ten years my father's junior, Nicola, with dark features and swarthy skin like his American cousin, was my father's alter ego. He and his wife, Concetta, live on the top floor of their hillside dwelling. Their three sons and one daughter reside with spouses and children on the floors beneath. Nicola seemed as bereft of demons as my father was rich in them.

The two cousins hit if off well and we spent days over sumptuous Sicilian meals of pasta, farm-raised lamb, and homemade wine, talking family, laughing, discovering uncanny coincidences—like both their firstborn sons are chemists. One afternoon my mother recounted the story of my first visit to Sicily, during which Nicola Tuzzolino called my parents in Pennsylvania, not realizing that it was three in the morning there. My mother, half asleep, yelled into the phone, "Hello!"

Nicola would reply, "Pronto!" Hellos and prontos went back and forth across the Atlantic several times until my mother woke up my father, saying, "It's Mussolini, he's calling collect from Sicily."

Nicola's offspring, all college educated, worked as professionals, while Nicola farmed several hundred acres of land including a parcel left behind by my father's father. Throughout our first week there, my father pestered Nicola to take him to see the farm. Nicola put it off, until, at last, one afternoon we drove the ten kilometers to see this fertile irrigated family land.

We spent hours touring the farm as Nicola proudly showed us the many crops that he had cultivated: pears, oranges, and apricots. We picked apples, persimmons, and small white and red grapes; we gathered tomatoes, eggplants, cucuzza, zucchini. Nicola's nephew Toto picked up runner vines and tied them to the wire fence and I picked a blade of wheat to take back to America. The land, golden in the scorching summer sun, stretched clean and clear for acres as far as the eye could see and in my depths I felt a sweetness and an unspoken family grief. In America, my father's progeny have fared well materially, but compared to the Tuzzolino clan, we are decidedly land-poor.

Perhaps it was this loss that led to the misunderstanding. "Where was my father's land?" my father innocently asked Nicola who was rankled and suspicious that we had come to reclaim what was once my grandfather's. Nicola defensively repeated the story we already knew—that my grandfather's mother had returned to Sicily after World War I and given Nicola's family the land in exchange for being taken care of until her death.

"No, no," my father winsomely protested, "you don't understand, it is your land, I don't want it. I only want to see where my father worked."

41

I understood what Nicola never could. My father wanted to harvest stories, salve a wound, not abscond with land. He wanted to understand another side of his titan of a father, the tough immigrant who let America's work ethic do him in by age 51. He wanted to imagine the youth who herded sheep, watered plants, slept on a hillock, chewed a blade of grass, bathed naked in the stream. My father was only nineteen when his father died, too young to down-size the god to human.

As Nicola shrugged and pointed off in some undefined distance, my father retreated from the subject. In no time, they were back on an even keel, Nicola back-slapping my father whom he respected deeply, not least of all for siring a passel of *bambini*. My parents enjoyed the remainder of their visit, attending many festive celebrations, including the Feast of San Calogero in Naro and the Feast of Jesus of Nazarene in San Giovanni-Gemini.

And my father even deigned to visit the grotto of Santa Rosalia in San Stefano. A beautiful but uppity woman of the Middle Ages, she resisted men's advances in favor of a hermit's contemplative life. Visitors must go down on bended knees to see her shrine. Kneeling, they must crawl through a narrow opening to pray at her altar. Even my father, former godhead, went down on bended knee.

Say what you want about the guy, he has come a long way.

3

Wilderness Begins at Home, 1995 (Breaking Bones to Touch the Sky)

(A tale of three Charlies in the heat of my heavy Zen practice; the way is still difficult; I still lift my feet, sit my bottom on a cushion, all that, and contemplate this: "The perfect way is without difficulty. Strive hard. This is the fundamental paradox of the way. One can be called upon to break one's bones, but we must also be reminded that the effort of following a path can itself lead one astray." —from a Gary Snyder lecture at Green Gulch Farm, Zen Center, 1988)

Six of us of varying strengths and minds are following a difficult path in the high Sierra. It is nearly 60 miles long with three passes over 12,000 feet high and includes an optional spur trail to the roof of the Lower Forty-Eight, 14,495-foot Mount Whitney.

Our party, containing three Charleses distinguished by different diminutives, consists of my partner, Dan, and me; my brother Chuck and his son, Chuckie; and Dan's two oldest siblings, Charlie and Julie. We embrace a 53-year age range, 14 to 67; a mean age of 38.5; and a median of 115.5. Our collective demographic intrigues me because within minutes of stepping on the trail each day we cease to be six. We are one.

Our trip starts in the eastern Sierra, which is markedly more dramatic than the range's west side. California may be divided attitudinally into north and south, but it is clearly nature's design to divide the state longitudinally. The spine of the Sierra Nevada splits the twain into east and west, a rift that is even more dramatic come winter. The east-west gates—Ebbetts, Sonora, and Tioga passes—are frozen shut, impassible by car for months.

Unlike the west side of the Snowy Range, which has the good sense to ascend in discreet increments, the east side doesn't bother with foothills. Its mountainous scaffold dominates the skyline, an understatement. The most confident of drivers squirm and weave along I-395 as the white-streaked scarp, with hanging snowfields and cloud-ringed crests, pulls eyes off the road.

Everything about mountain-making is terrifically exposed here. There is incriminating evidence of the vulcanism that fired up the granite "batholith," the faultblocking that tipped it, and the glaciers that gnawed it down. At a near right-angle ascent, the steep escarpment harbors serpentine canyons, sloping forests, rolling meadows, and wood-fringed lakes.

We are champing at the bit to avail ourselves of all of these. We meet at a campground in Independence, one of a string of small towns on the east side sheltered from time by their inhabitants, from weather by their geography. Just as abruptly as the Sierra ends, the Great Basin Desert begins. To the west of town, peaks froth with cloud and snow. To the east, superheated air moils over sagebrush in a grayish glare of convection. This has to be one of the most awesome geologic seams on the planet.

Our primitive dirt campground in Independence would seem drab minus the brilliant desert sun that glosses the tufts of greenery. In fact, I like its minimalism. In the afternoon, a hot wind sweeps through and the aspen tremble over the cold water in a creek rushing over rocks—a refreshing foot soak—and I am a wayfarer in a biblical scene.

"So you think you can keep up this time?" Charlie teases Dan, his little brother.

"If you don't stuff my pack with rocks," says Dan affectionately sidling up to his big brother. Dan is 10 and 12 years younger than his sister and brother who remind him of the hike they took in their youth in the northern Sierra. Dan was 10, pulling up the rear, ever-impatient to get wherever all this monotonous walking was taking them. Many years later now, Dan plays the protective sibling and carries the heaviest load. The three of them have a lifelong connection to the Sierra that I envy. My brother Chuck and I, refugees from New Jersey, are trying to catch up to them.

Our trip is a one-way or shuttle hike. We park two cars at the exit—at Whitney Portal—and all return in another car to the trailhead at Kearsarge Pass in Onion Valley where we will sleep tonight on a haunch of granite. As we prepare our knapsacks and divide up gear, we discover that a message from Julie to Dan to me got lost.

"I told you Julie was bringing the day food," Dan says with some irritation my way.

"No you didn't," I say, eyeing the high piles of nuts, dried fruit, peanut butter crackers, jerky, energy bars that will fill our daylong caloric needs.

"Looks like enough to feed a hungry Boy Scout troop," says Chuck.

This is a royal pain because you can't leave food behind in your car—you risk bear break-ins.

"Who's going to carry all this food?" Dan asks, bearing the brunt for the lapse in the chain of communication.

"The Boy Scouts," I'd like to say, but don't want add to the tension.

My own fear of heights—and mountains—makes the food glitch seem like a molehill. It is late in the season and we won't need crampons and ice axes at the passes. Still, as a flatlander from back east, I worry how challenging the snow field will be on high. But by morning, everyone is smiling and excited (if loaded with a bit too much edible cargo) and tensions give way to the thrill of getting into the glorious high country.

We set out at 8:30 a.m., letting distance fall between us as we climb to a meadow, then toward the first pass, Kearsarge, on a path of scree slashing the mountain back and forth, ever up. Big patches of snow sparkle along the trail and the way is truly long and hard. Soon we are beyond treeline and in sight of the pass, which is very narrow and one of the skimpiest I have seen, a mere nine square-foot flat area. We are surrounded by deep sky and can see in the distance the next set of sharp peaks. A dozen or so hikers scramble up the rocks to get to this first marker and to let the cool alpine air dry the sweat on their brows.

A brisk pace is well underway, proving our oneness. Pace is the result of group synergy. Though the mechanism at play is less apparent and deliberate, we are like drafting cyclists who form one beast. We pull each other in a psycho-physical slipstream. While cyclists ride with hair-trigger precision, the formula is more elusive for hikers. And we have not factored into the current equation the stride of a boy in his skate-boarding prime with that of a 67-year-old man who has just returned from the brink of death.

Eight months earlier, Charlie looked like a walking corpse. His swath of thick white hair turned to pitiful wisps, his sallow, thinned-out flesh hung like parchment on his skull and large frame. Dan and I visited him at his home in Salem, Oregon, and saw his ghost. He had been diagnosed with lymphoma and as with many cancers, the treatment seemed designed to do him in, rather than to heal. But he did heal and made a comeback in Charlie style. With his bright turquoise cap with ear flaps, he looks like Rocky the Flying Squirrel. His hair has grown in light brown and his wry sense of humor and what-me-worry attitude should see him into ripe old age. He retains only some residual numbness in his feet, his nerve endings having been damaged by the vicious chemotherapy.

Just before his cancer diagnosis, he, Dan, Julie, and I backpacked a stretch of the John Muir Trail, along which, one day, he recited to my enjoyment, Wordsworth's *Daffodils*. I remind him now with the first stanza:

I wander'd lonely as a cloud

That floats on high o'er vales and hills,

When all at once I saw a crowd,

A host, of golden daffodils;

I ask him to finish it, but, like Zorba who would not dance on demand, he says, "Later."

As Charlie crests the pass and sits on a rock, one hiker stares with great interest at his backpack. Sprouting from his pack are a metal cup, a shirt, a camera, various and sundry camp tools, and a spare pair of sneakers—Charlie hikes in sneakers, not expensive hiking boots like the rest of us. The hiker comments, "Man, I'd hate to see your bedroom," which brings a round of chuckles from everyone, including Charlie.

It is hard to fathom that Charlie, spry with a local boy's inbred sense of the Sierra backcountry, is just eight years my father's junior. They share the same first name and tendency toward big families—Charlie has 11 children (my father only 10, of which I am his fifth, Chuck his third)—the collateral effect of Irish and Italian Catholicism, perhaps. Yet their backgrounds can hardly be more diverse. A gallery of old family photos in mine and

Dan's home sums up that diversity. I refer to them as "Pioneers and Immigrants."

The "Immigrants": my parents and my Sicilian-born great-grand- and grandparents in their old-world accoutrements, shawls, long dresses, dark suits, somber faces. The "Pioneers": Dan's turn-of-the-century mother and her smiling sister and his grandfather, in whom I have always seen Charlie's mischievous grin. The grandfather (a Taaffe, rhymes with safe) in his western attire—shirt, neckerchief, and suspenders—embodies frontier spirit.

Dan, Julie, and Charlie, Taaffes, are direct descendants of the Murphys, touted as California's "First Irish Family." In 1844, Great-Great-Great-Grandfather Martin Murphy, who had left his home country because Catholics were not allowed an education, arrived in California by wagon train at what would become known as Donner Lake. (The Murphys' successful trans-Sierra crossing has been eclipsed by the more sensational Donner Party.) The charming Sierra foothill town, Murphys, is named after Martin's sons Daniel and John, Dan's great uncles, who were among the first to struck it rich there in gold in 1849, riches they wisely turned into land.

I enjoy exploring the outdoors with the (many) Taaffes whose family mythology is deeply embedded in the mountains and the wilderness. They have *terroir*, that difficult-to-translate term, usually applied to the famous Bordeaux red wines. My Cassell's French dictionary translates the word as *native tang, to smack of the soil*, which sums it up perfectly. The way their eyes define a ridge, pick out a wild grass or flower, or study a river course betray a deeply bred sense of place that I have been trying to cultivate.

Aspiring to *terroir*, Chuck and I have roots that go back less than 100 years—to April 16, 1903. That's the day our paternal Grandfather Vincenzo Cusumano arrived from Sicily at Ellis Island, New York, in the third class section of the German ship *Palatia*. With purpose full and clear, he pursued the American Dream—to own a home, get a free public education for his children, have some disposable income. He achieved all three before he died at the age of 51, a year younger than Chuck at the time of this trip. His death certificate attributes death to "natural causes."

I met Dan and his family about the time I had a read a life-changing essay by Gary Snyder called *Good, Wild, and Sacred*. "We have no one to teach us which parts of the landscape were once thought to be sacred," Snyder wrote, lamenting our collective loss of a sense of place. Snyder put his finger on an unnamed grief I had been experiencing. I realized that, after having a rather stable childhood (albeit in a place I never felt was worthy of my dreams) I had just completed my 23rd move in 19 years. It never occurred to me that I could actually miss New Jersey, which I had left nearly 20 years before. Snyder's essay inspired me to start walking the paths I found right where I was. Walking the land, says Snyder, is a veritable exercise in "expanding consciousness." So, it happened that I began to make seasonal forays into the wilderness around the West—Big Sur, the Sierra, Death Valley, Joshua Tree, Mount Tamalpais—and to change my address much less often.

As we tramp up and down the long, sinuous trail toward Vidette Meadow on our second day and toward the foot of Mount Forrester on the third day, I try to hone my power of observation, taking cues from Julie. Dan points to a fat tree and she notes the type of cones, the length and number of needles per packet, the pattern of bark. She keys a limber pine for us. She points to the stunning mauve flower, mountain heather, to penstemon, golden groundsel, a water-loving tiger lily, shooting stars, and wild onion in a meadow. The nature books Julie carries are worth their weight in what they add to our trip. With each new name I learn for living wild things I feel my consciousness expand, my roots take hold. It cultivates the connection I crave.

In fascinating contrast is my brother Chuck, a Vietnam vet who still has some marching soldier in him, and who hardly notices the world of flowers or vegetation. His connection to the wild is no less deep. He immerses himself with equal concentration in precise readings made with his compass, altimeter, topos, and GPS (global positioning system). They are parallel universes, Chuck's and Julie's, and I love the moments, feeling the breadth and depth of our universe, when I am a part of both at once. Indeed, wilderness begins at home.

By the time we reach the layover at the foot of Mount Forrester, the pace is wreaking havoc on our group

51

serenity. Some of us, unhappy campers, are on the verge of drowning in the "pooled energy" that is overly inundated with the pace of the fastest hikers, Chuck and Chuckie. At the end of this day's long toil, we are all distraught for different reasons.

Charlie is experiencing serious fatigue and, we later learn, a great deal of pain in his nerve-damaged feet. Dan is concerned about the over-exhaustion of Julie and Charlie. I am anxious about the next morning's climb over snow-laden Forrester. And Chuck is concerned about Chuckie, for whom there is no middle speed between sprinting and being still. He doesn't want his son to have a negative experience on his first backpacking trip.

We are breaking our bones to touch the sky on a path with too much effort.

I wonder sometimes about the burden of my brother's name. Charles Anthony, anglicized from the Italian, Calogero Antonio, echoes back through the ages of our male forebears in Sicily. It was riveting to see the name with my own eyes, handwritten in cursive many times on the yellowed pages of registers in the municipal building of my grandfather's medieval village. The importance of being Charles, impressed upon my brother by our father amounted to *Never say die*.

Charlie, the elder who can say *die*, prevails this evening. He plops down and says, "I'm not going another step," which foils Chuck's idea to get us just a wee bit closer to the pass. We are near treeline with a broad view of Center Basin. Stubby trees sweep up the bowl like dry ingredients. Julie spots columbine and elephant's head clover. Charlie just passes out for the night without eating dinner and the rest of us eat and turn in early—sleeping with food in our tents, a big no-no.

Up before sunrise, we skip breakfast, a mistake, to get a jump on the long trudge upward to 13,000-foot Mount Forrester. At about 12,000 feet I am hit with a nasty case of altitude sickness, my first ever. So is Chuckie. My stomach churns on the few handfuls of granola I've eaten en route and my head starts to split in two in slow motion. Dramamine makes me sicker. I can barely make the scramble up a final 50-foot-high pile of boulders only to be at the start of the long high traverse over snow. If I slip off the trail, I will slide way down the mountain into a bowl. Luckily, the sun has beaten the snow to a soft slush. Sickness takes my mind off fear. Weakly, I put one foot in front of the other and cross the blinding snow that intensifies my headache. Hikers gather, gleeful and triumphant, on the far side of the traverse. But Chuckie and I have to get to lower altitude.

At the bottom of the pass, we lie in the sun, sleep, and awake feeling much better. We hike down the open Diamond Mesa and on to Tyndall Creek, all meeting up in the designated third set of trees, our address for the night. We need those tall trees, after all the spare biological detail of a day above treeline. Rock has beauty, to be sure, but we humans are closer in evolutionary age to trees.

Dan is relieved that Charlie, though quite tired, does not crash without dinner this evening. In fact as he whistles a tune I don't recognize, he cooks it for us—a tempting turkey tetrazzini. Next morning, we linger in camp, indulging the best time of day in the wilderness. We set out leisurely, crossing our first high water at Wright and Wallace creeks, bathing in the latter—quickly, as we are eaten by mosquitoes. And then we turn our thoughts to Mount Whitney.

But not all of us will summit. Chuck, correctly reading his son's cues, decides to split and finish the trip at Chuckie's sprint speed. They hike out to Whitney Portal in less than half the time it will take the rest of us. I'm sorry to see my side of the family go, but all of us— Charlie and Julie, not least of all—breathe a sigh of relief. The pace will get sane.

We spend the next night, our seventh day on the trail, at lovely Crabtree Meadow where we have the most coveted of luxuries in the backcountry, a fire ring, plenty of downed fire wood, and spring water running from a pipe. The only other tenants are a father-daughter team who are ambitiously traversing the Sierra west to east. The next day takes us past Timberline Lake, then Guitar Lake, and finally to Hitchcock Lakes where we'll sleep before ascending Whitney. After dinner, Dan and I stroll around one of the shallow lakes and see dozens of frogs and tadpoles in the limpid water. These metamorphosing amphibians are a powerful icon of my New Jersey summers and I dream that night:

I am holding a little girl for whom I feel affection and concern and singing her a song, *If ever I should leave you. . .* I feel a deep conviction that I will care for and be responsible for this neglected child. As I lay her on a bed, I see her legs are like a mermaid's, very shapely, like the many tadpole legs I had seen in Hitchcock Lakes.

When I awaken I know this baby-morphing-into-woman represents the renewal of the spirit that takes place in the wilderness. It can—and does—take place anywhere, any time. Whether on a wooded trail or an asphalt road, life is a step-by-step journey with its ups and downs and transformations. Still, experiencing rebirth amid ancient forest and rock fonts of pure snowmelt, is truly *wild*.

As if part of an initiation ceremony, high winds career down the pass all night and buffet our tents. They help us rise early next morning. My adrenaline runs high. I feel no hunger, but don't make the mistake of having no breakfast. I eat cold food, enough to stave off sickness. Our pace is slow and steady. Dan and I take the lead as we climb to the intersection where hikers leave their packs—an honor system—before making the grand ascent to the summit. The last two miles are on a sort of catwalk grooved securely into rock with long drops on either side and intoxicating views. We pass four of what we dub "picture windows," sudden openings in the stone façade where we see far to the east and deeply, dizzily into Owens Valley, more than a mile down. To the west we see the ragged peaks of the Great Western Divide. Time stops and space takes over at these heights.

Rather, time dilates—it becomes not linear, nor circular, but "webular." I see clearly in all directions at once; past, present, and future are artificial distinctions; the interrelationships I have with plant, animal, and rock are one continuous web. A pile of talus is a living record of fire in the earth, plant succession, geological forces all at once; gravity is one with the rivers it pulls, with the earth they score as it spins on its axis, just as the past that shapes my smile or frown lines or gait is not separate from them. The webular universe looks the same in all directions, a vision that arises naturally when the eyes and brain adjust to the absence of man's artifice in the wilderness.

The summit of Whitney would seem unspectacular minus its loftiness. It's a chaotic field of scree and talus, rock quarried down to size by weather and Earth's restlessness. It is startling to come upon an old stone structure up there, the Smithsonian, built in 1909 for astronomers studying solar radiation. And there is this indulgence—a pit toilet. It has no ceiling but walls that rise to shoulder height, prompting hikers to call it "throne with a view."

Intrepid mountaineers climb the long technical routes of three spires of Mount Whitney, but most visitors come up for a long day hike from the east side, through Whitney Portal. Some, like our party, take a week or longer to pack in and approach the peak from the west. Whichever way one comes, Whitney is "the single most sought after summit in North America," write Stephen F.

Porcella and Cameron M. Burns in their book, *Climbing California's Fourteeners.*

By mid-morning, the peak's broad appeal is all too apparent to Dan and me as hikers arrive in a steady stream, reminding us that we are a day's walk from civilization. One of those hikers rounding the bend makes us happy. Charlie's turquoise cap with earflaps and his wry smile precede him. Julie, stretched beyond her limit, has remained at the pass intersection among the hikers' packs to rest. Charlie, with his tingling, painful toes, is stretched beyond his limit, too. But this could be his (and ours, for that matter) last chance to gaze out at the deep valleys, at the generous and magnificent views his earthly home offers.

My head begins to throb from the altitude, so I leave Dan and his big brother to have some precious time alone and head down. Julie is in good spirits considering that, had she not been pushed so hard for a week, she'd have summited, too. She gives me the name for the most beautiful flower I've seen to date in the Sierra. We'd seen it since Mount Forrester, but here at Whitney the rock-loving blossom is prolific. The sky blue cluster of supple but dainty petals is hydrangea-like with fern-like foliage. "Sky pilot," says Julie, having found it in her book. *Sky pilot.* I love its name, which instantly makes me sing the old Animals song, *skyyyyy, pilot, how high can you fly? You never, never, never, touch the sky.*

We hike down, long and steep, to Outpost campsite for our last night. We pass many beautiful Jeffrey trees and sniff their hint of vanilla. We're all exhausted but Charlie is beyond the pale. Dan and I won't know how bad, until days after the trip. Fortunately, the next morning is short and we make it to Whitney Portal trailhead where we get our first showers in more than a week and, at the general store, pancakes bigger than a Frisbee. Renewed within and without now, we are all in fine form, especially Charlie, whose sense of pride and accomplishment are palpable. It is his last walk in the woods and it will always remind me of the paradoxical qualities of a flower—soft and blue, it thrives on the rock-hardest of mountains. Charlie Taaffe, 1928—1998.

4

Fine China does the Big Easy, 2001

I have found backpack trips into the mountains a good way to reconnect with my brothers. Going into the wilderness with my five sisters would be redundant. Together, we are a wilderness unto ourselves. *Leave no trace* might have been a euphemism for our Sicilian father's subzero-tolerance warning to men.

I have chosen New Orleans as the venue where my five sisters and I will meet to celebrate my birthday. Its wet, dewy tropical urban wilds befits the feminine principle. And I know that my sisters and I can blend seamlessly with a city renowned for celebrating the human impulse, hedonistic and otherwise.

Before going, we exchange emails regarding a famous case, in which a court of law found nine Italians not guilty of the murder of the Irish New Orleans Chief of Police. But anti-Italian immigrant sentiment was strong in 1891 and a mob lynched 11 Italians—who were still in police custody. Our emails stream over the Net:

—*Should we get mad or even for what they did to our goombahs?*

—*I'm packin'. The digibeta with top Sony stuff. Don say nuttin ta nobody*

—*Dose rebels aint never seen nothin like us before.*

—*I'm wit ya. 'Sides, I'm only doin' it fer my babies!*

59

— *Forget the guns, cannoli's mightier than the sword. They don't do right by us with the food, though, we forget the cannoli, get out the swords.*

My five sisters are flying in from the east. I'm flying in from San Francisco. The Sister Ghetto, as I refer to us collectively, spreads over five different states. Only Grace and Terry live in the same one, New Jersey, 75 miles apart. Tina's in Pennsylvania; Donna's in New York; Lisa's in Maryland. There is a drug, *Sorella Euphoria*, maybe. It has heady highs and edgy withdrawal. Why else do you think we don't live closer?—we'd be narcotized half the time.

We're meeting at the McKendrick Breaux Inn, 1474 Magazine Street in the Lower Garden district. My sisters have entrusted me with all arrangements because I am the most traveled. I almost said most worldly. But in the sister mosaic, I am the most *other*-worldly. I've wandered the farthest on earth and also the farthest spiritually. Marriage and child-bearing have slipped my mind. I've lived with a man for eight years. And I've brought Zen Buddhism's lexicon into an intractably Roman Catholic family. The sisters, from the sidelines, have always cheered my boldness.

I'm the first one to arrive, anticipating my high. I notice that parts of the 'hood are shabby, but our block, near Race, has character. While I await their arrival, I plot our route to the Quarter. I eat raw oysters, crawfish étouffé at a tourist joint. I wait and wait at the Breaux, which was built in 1860 and renovated by Mr. Eddie, the owner. The three-story brick building has high ceilings, chandeliers, floor-length drapery, period antiques, and polished wood floors. I know these details by heart at 11 p.m. when my five sisters finally ring the bell.

They're all laughing loudly and explaining at once. They went to 1414 Magazine Street. They unloaded all their luggage onto the sidewalk. Knowing my minimalist persuasion, they wondered what kind of joint did I pick. The place was cold, dark, and uninviting. The windows were boarded up. Finally, Grace, the most logic-driven among us, had the presence of mind to check the address. Back in the taxi went all the luggage. My sisters do not travel lightly. I talk to them about this. I may as well be whistlin' Dixie.

We have two rooms. Terry, Lisa, and I take the one on the third floor with sloping attic ceiling. Terry, the oldest sister, is the Earth Mother to whom I owe my ability to blaze trails without recrimination. Born Maria Theresa after Dad's sainted mother, Terry dutifully started delivering the much awaited grandchildren at age 19. As kids, Grace and I loved watching Terry sneak kisses with her boyfriends. She went steady with Paul for a long time and they would take us to mass on Sundays then for cream and jelly doughnuts afterward, which we brought home to have with coffee. (We had all fasted for hours in those days in order to receive Holy Communion. Even to this day, I love the physiological effects of fasting in the morning then zapping my system with caffeine and sweets, thank-you Catholic upbringing). But Terry married John who became like a fifth son to our family and

61

brother to us kids. Their nuclear marriage lasted a good, solid 20 years (and through five children). Following its meltdown, Terry blossomed into a psychologist. While Terry's practiced in the art of illogic and the shadow side of the Family, Lisa is an unlikely mix of sound logic (second to Grace's) and hair-trigger tears. It does not escape us that she cries only twice during our trip, after talking by phone to her little girls, who are three and seven.

We put the smokers, Grace, Tina, and Donna, in the carriage house, across the courtyard. Good, I would end up shaking my head at Tina's thongs and asking her why she needs 39 pairs of black shoes. I would try to convey to her my infinite wisdom about how wearing those vaginal irritant straps is tied to an unexamined need to please the patriarchy. I would try to find simple words to say this, because as Donna notes, Tina, who has lived deep in Pennsylvania Dutch country since some single-digit age "speaks another mother tongue." Tina would stare back at me through kohl-blackened eyes and say "Panty line."

Tina has so much of what Terry, à la Jung, might call *puella* that I often think of her as the baby. But Donna is two years younger. Despite being a material girl like Tina, Donna has some old-soul wisdom and the creative intellect that drives my spur-of-the-moment calls to her East Village pad. Tall, thin, and dark, she can simulate the swagger of Jane Russell or May West and the intelligent, tipsy humor of Dorothy Parker. Donna cuts to life's irony the way Grace does to logic, Lisa to tears, Terry to analysis, Tina to the fashion faux pas. Like me, she has no children and is married to someone who, for better or worse, has left her autonomy—and irony—intact.

Grace, with whom I shared my bed the first 18 years of her life, would be in my room, but for her rare and dubious distinction of having taken up smoking at age, 49. I don't know why. She doesn't either. She and I were so close as kids, we answered to each other's name. Born a year and four days after me, Grace, like me, is classic middle kid—we learned early on how to fly under the parental radar and enjoyed some of the best years of our lives anonymously rebelling in high school. One of my life's earliest disappointments was her marriage (a rather hasty one) at eighteen. I left for the West Coast a couple of years later.

Our being together is such a destination in itself that we lounge over coffee Friday morning in the bright dining room, lost in *Sorella Euphoria*. I take it upon myself to remind the girls why we've come and by late morning the sisters are loosed upon the Big Easy. The city is great backdrop for our irrepressible kibitzing. Our first walk is upriver on Charles Street with its Queen Anne revival mansions and historic residences. Every time I arc out into the street to look downriver for a streetcar, the five sisters unconsciously mimic me as if we were shackled to one another or playing follow the leader.

"I didn't say, Simon Sez," I say, arcing back onto the sidewalk with five adult women in tow.

63

A man with a brooding look is following us. There is only one thing to do. Tina and Donna confront him— "Can we help you?" He turns out to be a German tourist who speaks little English. Still, they order him to snap our picture in front of a wrought iron gated mansion. Then we hop the Charles streetcar to storm the French Quarter.

There at Jackson Square, where everyone with a claim to real or imagined Gypsy blood is set up to read palms, we drive the bargaining. We find a blond man wearing a babushka and a pirate's earring who claims to be half Sicilian. He gives us a group discount for our combined tarot. The reading, however, drones and our own futures seem dull.

"We can't just abandon him," says soft-touch Terry, out of his earshot.

"Offer the guy severance pay," says Donna. "He'll still make out." Which we do. Which he takes.

We then get inducted into the wash band of a fat lady street artist, playing bells, tambourines, spoons, and washboard. We laugh so hard at our own silliness that other tourists give us wide berth. We don't help the fat lady's business any.

We walk over to Uglesevich's, one of the restaurants mentioned in guidebooks that really does embody old New Orleans. Its exterior is buff colored wood, its small, tight interior is like a bar that spread into a restaurant. It reminds us of Spirito's, an old pizzeria joint that's been dishing Italian food in Elizabeth Port, New Jersey since the early 19th century. We drink two bottles of red wine that we brought with us, during the long wait for our po' boys and shrimp cakes.

Lisa entertains us with the story of her daughter: "When Anna was two and half years old she asks me about her different body parts. She points and wants to know what each part was called. When she gets to her vagina, I tell her that's what it is called. She's quick to point out that men don't have 'faginas.' I agree and tell her that men have penises. About two weeks later I'm talking to Vadj about getting a wedding gift, a piece of fine china for the bride. Anna hears me and says, 'I have a fine china.' When I question her further she says, "I have a fine china and daddy has peanuts!""

This sets us off like church chimes:

—*Anna has to put her fine china in a hope chest.*

—*She can't take it out til she's married, right?*

—*Does she get to show off her fine china to prospective husbands?*

—*After they're married, will they eat off the fine china?*

—*How did Daddy feel being sized up as 'peanuts'?*

A bald man in a blue suit, a lawyer, moves in and sits down with us. Joe Marcal is his name and his accent reminds me that John Kennedy Toole calls New Orleans "Hoboken by the Gulf of Mexico," in his Pulitzer-prize-winning novel, *A Confederacy of Dunces.* Are we related to a local Judge Cusimano? asks Joe. No relation, but Joe wants to tell us how corrupt this local judge, a Republican is. Joe talks a lot and clearly has sex on his mind.

A sexual charge in the Sister Hood recalls an incident some years back, Grace, Donna, and I were out jogging in Roosevelt Park, in Edison, New Jersey, near Grace's former suburban digs. A man jumps out of the woods, pulls his limp penis through his red shorts, and wags it at us. The sisters act swiftly to this rude gesture as he runs into hiding. "Hey, you! Coward! Pea-size balls! C'mon back and try that again! We spread out and block his obvious escape routes, thinking three of us could tackle him. Grace runs and calls the police who are there in minutes. We actually find and arrest the guy—a wet spot on his shorts. Grace and I go to court to testify. At the lawyer's request, we drop charges in exchange for the exhibitionist's working with a psychologist. The guy, it turns out, works as a security guard across from Grace's workplace and has a wife and child.

He looked so young, timid, and vulnerable at the hearing. I like to believe the Sisters helped restore him to acts more beneficial to the greater sisterhood. We felt sorry for him. Kind of the way I now feel sorry for Joe as Tina and Donna, animated by the wine, are on a par with his b.s.ing and wear him down with steady, irrelevant questions.

We show up on Royal Street in time for the cemetery voodoo tour. The brochure promises "profoundly moving decay." A group of 20 is assembled to tour the above-ground tombs in the city that sits below sea level and keeps dry by the grace of its elaborate levees. The crumbling crypts turn the cemetery into a labyrinth. But it's at the voodoo temple over on Rampart Street where things get interesting. The guide prepares the group for the possibility that voodoo Priestess Miriam can be long winded as she waxes on about nothing much (a little New Age, a little Old Age, he explains).

The Sisters go into a huddle. If someone wants to slip away, she will ask, "Where's the cannoli?" Then we'll slip out one by one, unnoticed.

The temple is a small dark room connected to a storefront like an old head shop, with lots of kitsch and voodoo dolls stuffed with the Spanish Moss that hangs from the old oak trees. Out in back is a grassy yard with some farm animals. The backs of neighboring houses enclose the yard. Presently, Priestess Miriam steps into the yard where the crowd awaits her. She has thrown a long aquamarine tie-dyed smock over her black turtleneck. She wears sandals, hoop earrings, and a black kerchief to hold her hair back.

She begins grandly, "What did you bring in your heart for me today?"

"Curiosity," I say.

"Fun," Terry says.

She rants on for a few minutes about not being curious. "Curiosity killed the cat," she says.

"Satisfaction brought it back," the Sisters answer as if someone pushed a cue button. Feeling upstaged, Miriam rants on more. Some guy interrupts, "I want to know how you got to be you."

"Let me warn all against wanting to be me. I was born in Mississippi and picked cotton . . . You don't want to be me." An interesting start, but then she rambles and rambles.

Where's the cannoli? I whisper to Grace and the question goes discreetly down the line to Lisa to Tina to Donna and to Terry. Perfect. We have positioned ourselves near the back door of her shop to slip out. Grace, most eager to leave, turns around and instead of going through the storefront, goes right through the adjacent door into Miriam's temple, her sanctuary.

Before I can whisper to Grace to get the hell out of there, Priestess Miriam's face goes two shades darker. She interrupts her lecture and says, "Excuse me, Miss!"

Grace turns around bewildered. "Where do you think you're going?" asks Miriam with indignation. Grace is speechless. The dark priestess banishes us all to the far corner of the courtyard.

"You all go stand over there by the goats and pigs!" she points. We do not dare disobey. We move, a 12-legged sister-pede, to the back of the yard. We're stuck. We fuel her lecture though.

"Who's not married among you?" she asks with hellfire and brimstone in her voice and coal-black eyes. Two of us raise our hands.

"You wriggled out of it, humph!"

"It's an unnatural state," I egg her on.

"I wouldn't want to be your mother," she says. Her nostrils flare like Dizzy Gillespie's trumpet.

"Hey!" We yell from our corner. "Our mother loves us!"

"She says the rosary every day for us!"

"Yeah!"

"Yeah!"

Miriam says something indecipherable about the rosary and continues her chastisement after a fashion. Then, inexplicably, she abridges her talk and lets the crowd tour her temple, perhaps the better to hasten our departure.

It is a dim, tight space, chock full of altars of every sort, with everything from windup toys to mini bottles of Jack Daniels, textiles of every warp and weave, colored plastic stones. We are quiet and behave. Terry, my sister the psychologist, apologizes to Miriam in the temple and asks if she "wants to talk about it." Miriam sweeps away the very suggestion with her hand and a grimace. "Don't apologize," she says. Donna and I, pious pagans, buy one little tchotchke each to put on our own home altars.

To Miriam's relief, we leave. We rush down Rampart weaving our way over to Big Muddy for the paddleboat ride. Then, at Acme Oyster House in the Quarter, we order gumbo, jambalaya with andouille, and crawfish. Our talk reaches below the surface this third day together. Masked by the din of clanging dishes, someone broaches one of our most open secrets. A baby born out of wedlock to one of us is a young woman now. We could try to find her and bring her into the family. A fist bangs the table. The lost child (LC) will not be discussed.

This grieves us all—within our sister mythology we have no boundaries. More intriguing than our difference is our sameness—eerily demonstrated when three of us bought the same exotic peasant blouse in three different states. We are not six pieces of fine china, but a whole set, Judy Chicago designed. *We* have borne 14 children—3 boys, and 11 girls. LC, born to us at age 15, was given up for adoption. We are more at peace with the loss of a girl, who died of a birth defect at one week. We have married seven times, divorced three times. We have five B.A.s, three M.A.s, one beauty operator's license, one nursing degree, one marriage-and-family counseling certificate. We are our mother's daughter, at once overly submissive by default. We have the most polarized of love for a father who at his worst, in a drunken rage, gave us one black eye and at his best, gave us arms infinitely protective. He gave us night terrors and impossible dreams. This is the amalgam people see when we are together.

Silently, each of us remembers where she was when she heard about LC's conception and birth. LC's mother was safe in the home of the minister (with LC's father) when the good clergyman called my parents. I stood on the threshold of one sister's home thinking, "Fucking-A, I waited until I could get birth control." Another sister went with Mom to the hospital the day LC was delivered. An African American woman took her hand and led her away past dozens of staring strangers. "Cuuurrriosity killed the cat," she repeated, singing the first couple of syllables, unlike Miriam.

LC came at the darkest moment in our family history, during our father's downward spiral to drinking. While everyone else tried to apply logic to the situation, our over-the-top father sobbed with uncontrollable remorse about losing "my flesh and blood." His drama proved prophetic. A deep sense of loss, with 30 grandchildren to date (not including LC) to remind us one is missing, bears down year after year. What is she like, which one does she most take after? I find it hard to believe any adopted kid out in the world has a bigger, more intact biological family than LC. I wish that one day all the constricting religious and social mores that took her from us vanish and she finds us and her place on this old, gnarled family tree. Her spot is waiting.

There's only one thing to do for shame and guilt. Drink too much spirits. The rainy afternoon encourages this as we retreat inside the Breaux, lying on the bed in the smokers' room, kibbitzing too hard, empty wine bottles on their sides. Not all of us share in the excess; some of us brood, some of us observe the family shadow. Some of us watch rain drops find their random and chaotic trail down glass panes. All of us await for that safe place of cohesion—our default mode—to return.

By evening, we are back on the same wavelength—we came to New Orleans to party. We dress up real sharp and put on jewelry to step out. I wear make-up, which pleases Tina to no end. We make the scene at Susan Spicer's Herbsaint, where we ham it up for photographs that strangers snap for us. I lie across the other five on a leather couch with an emerald green feather boa thrown around us. More than once, we answer the question, "Are you all sisters?" What was your first clue?

On our last evening in New Orleans, we stop by Pat O'Brien's for a few Hurricanes. Tina gives me the evil eye for not letting some guys buy us a round. This, from a successful businesswoman who runs her own beauty salon. Grace has reservations about our younger sisters' trifling with men's attentions. I tell her it is a harmless reflex, a defense mechanism acquired by them early on.

"Did you run that theory by Terry?" asks Grace.

"Yeah, she appointed me Head Shrink tonight," I say.

We head over to Bourbon Street where men in hungry droves roar as women flash their breasts from balconies. The music blossoms loud and electric out of every doorway— jazz and blues to country, disco and rock. Drunken revelers in good spirits are everywhere. At the strip joints, women dance as silhouettes behind frosted glass windows. But the most beautiful woman hawking the street is a he, at a place called "Men will be girls." *Laisser les bon temps rouler.*

Before turning in, we take a cab to the Trolly Stop on St. Charles for some deep-fried diner food. When we're done the waiter asks a cabbie at another table if he'll take us back to our inn.

"Can I finish my coffee?" he asks us.

Sure," we say, ready to nod in place. The cabbie, wearing a French beret, stops to talk to a clutch of cops at a nearby table, then drives us back to the Breaux. He won't accept our money. We insist. "No, I can't," he says, "the Sergeant told me not to."

"We oughta bury da hatchet," Donna says. All agreed.

As we slip between our sheets, we wonder when and where we'll do this all again.

5

How Bears Take Their Coffee, 1996

Each summer, Chuck and I meet on common ground on our backpack trips in the Sierra Nevada. Out in the rarefied air of gods' country, we avoid, with only an occasional slip, discussing our opposing political views.

This is not to say we don't argue. We argue relentlessly.

But that's because bickering was how we learned to relate growing up in our populous family. First of all, who had time for niceties like waiting one's turn to speak or speaking in a conversational tone over eleven others? But more urgently, to not quibble was to not have an identity. The standard modus operandi was to have the last word, on the most innocuous topic—how to dunk biscotti in your coffee or how to eat macaroni with a fork and spoon. To not pick an argument even over moot points— who was buried in Grant's tomb—was to fall down in the process of individuation, a demand ever looming in a big family. You did not budge an inch on your stance even when you were well beyond the point of caring if you were right or wrong about which came first, chicken or egg.

With a plenitude of subjects to evoke that no-win childhood paradigm in the backcountry, who needed heated political discussions?

One such subject with radioactive content was the drinking of unfiltered water. I steadfastly held that it was safe to drink the bracing snowmelt of streams at 10,000 feet or higher and I proved so by gulping this refreshing tonic to my heart's content.

"You don't know what you're missing," I'd smack my lips.

"You just wait," Chuck would taunt, pumping away on his state-of-the-art water filter, "there's always a first time." The specter of giardia (the parasite present in streams in very few parts per million, due to wild and domestic animals) would hang briefly in the air. I'd imagine the intestinal cramps that chain you to the toilet. But then I'd feel bound by the family code of expression.

"If that hi-tech equipment of yours gets any heavier, you're gonna need a U-Haul to get it here," I would chide him mercilessly about the unnecessary weight of the filtering system. I had the last word on that one. Or so I thought until a few weeks after our trip I opened the mail. He sent me an ad from *Backpacker* magazine for a water filter. A beautiful wild coyote was aiming a thick yellow ribbon of urine right into a high mountain stream, all crystal and pristine, like the ones I drink from.

"I just have to outrun you," Chuck says, the old joke about bears. But Sierra bears, unless you come between a mother and her cub, don't want to harm us. Another contentious subject is bears and food. Of course, we agree that bears must not get our food. Never mind the fine the park service would slap on us for corrupting bear nature. Who wants to lose any of her rations deep in the woods? We hang our stash, using the recommended counterbalance system from a tree—the branch must be some 15

75

feet high and you have to position the bag so the bear can't reach it from the trunk (which he can and will climb) or by swiping at it from the ground with his razor-sharp talons. On popular trails the park service has installed metal food storage boxes, which backpackers love, as the tree system is proving more and more not to be bearproof. Bears, our Sierra Nevada black bears in particular, are smart and ever on a steep learning curve (no pun intended).

But above treeline, about 10,000 feet in the Sierra, there are no trees worth their puny limbs. No worries, I say. Bears are less likely to roam that high anyway. So I have been known to hide my vacuum-sealed food in my tent with me as I sleep. Most bears—OK, there are exceptions—do not want to hassle with humans. I take my chances. It's a crap-shoot, as with the drinking of unfiltered water. As with many things in life. But Chuck is totally opposed to sleeping with food in the tent because the rangers say not to.

"You never question authority," I tease him.

"You're gonna get mauled one of these days, just wait," he says ominously.

"You don't always have to follow the party line, use your head." Then, under my breath: "Such a Republican."

And so far the bears have not gotten to our food. That is with the exception of one time, which proved us both right and both wrong. I'll explain.

First you have to know that coffee is another subject loaded with bicker potential. Sure, I'll eat and relish the most mundane dried foods out back. I'll forego the wine and spirits with my evening meal and all manner of dining pleasure. But in the morning I must have my Peet's coffee, the San Francisco Bay Area's finest fair-trade beans. I carry my own stash—Sierra Dorada blend, what else? A chalice-like mug and the small Melitta filter get attached to a strap of my backpack. Chuck drinks rotgut and I do not spare him my feelings on those American coffee-filled teabags. Pure acid. How could we have come from the same parents? I lament. He says my coffee is too bitter and not worth the extra weight.

Yes it is, I say.

No, it isn't, he counters.

It is.

It ain't.

Neither one will quit.

Now cross my coffee with bears, who have an incredibly developed sense of smell. You might think you'd get a situation with contention to fuel a walk along the entire Pacific Crest Trail. But what you get are two campers who make Goldilocks look brilliant.

This one fateful summer, Chuck and I were out backpacking in the southern Sierra, the loftiest part of the Range of Light—it holds most of the shiny, snow-laden peaks over 14,000 feet, including Mount Whitney, the Roof of the Lower 48 at 14,940 feet. It was our second time out doing the Rae Lakes Loop, the same route that only a few years earlier we had covered for our first backpack trip. Oh, we had made our share of mistakes on that debut trek—carried too much weight in food, which we didn't eat. Unbelievably—fearing that a lack of home-style food would dampen Chuck's appetite for the wilderness—I had packed angel hair pasta, Parmesan cheese, olive oil, sundried tomatoes, canned tuna, oh my god, way wrong foods to carry. We had not filled our water bottles before a long dry stretch that nearly dehydrated us. Our Whisper Lite cook stove was the wrong model and its pump failed us at altitude. So we had no hot water, hence no morning coffee, a terrible mistake that shall never be repeated.

We also had the brazen company of one *Ursus americanus* at one campsite. This cub, all chestnut and sleek, would pad up a steep slope when we made noise to scare him, then noiselessly return, still curious. He kept returning, sniffing for our food, even though the nearby meadow was a pantry of wild food—pale blue elderberries, huckleberries, and Sierra currants. We had to break camp and begin our final miles in the dark.

He was not the beast who got our food.

We had also experienced our first epiphany on the Rae Lakes Loop. We were like two inner-city kids loosed in the wilds on an outward bound survival trip. Mid-way through the trip, atop 12,000-foot Glenn Pass, we sat on a rock to rest and pull in the thin cool air.

"Listen," my brother said.

"To what?"

"Listen," he said impatiently.

"What, I don't hear a thing."

"That's what. The sound of silence."

It was all new to us—the bold granite formations, lakes so shining they could blind, a dramatic glacier-scoured canyon, thrushes and chickadees charting course from a wildflower-rimmed meadow, and sky so deep it seemed to have the loft of velvet. We hiked the 45-mile trail pretty quickly though. So, in the spirit of Bill Murray in *Groundhog Day*, we decided to go back, experienced and wiser, to do it right and savor it slowly. But this second time out we were plagued by thunderstorms, which are not conducive to slow savoring. Trying to beat the next cloudburst spurred us on to a forced march.

Our last full day was one hell of a long one, during which we donned all our raingear and prayed that our backpack frames didn't act like conducting rods as we dodged lightning bolts. We reached Junction Meadow along Bubbs Creek for our last night's campsite during a break in the rain.

"There were bear boxes here last time," Chuck said with the sangfroid of Albert Schweitzer greeting Dr. Livingston. We had just spent more than half the hours in a day hiking some 20 rigorous miles—not 20 city-street miles, but 20 rocky-path, altitudinous, extra-long mountain miles.

"Park service wants you to call 'em 'food storage' boxes not bear boxes," I said, equally dispassionate about our day's accomplishment.

"I don't care if you call them jack-squat boxes. My legs are so beat, they think the dirt caked on them is doing the walking."

"Yeah? Well, I'm so exhausted even my sweat is complaining."

"Tell me about it."

"I just did."

Our movement was as circular and aimless as our conversation. Anyone watching us from up on the granite ridge would see two backpacks slowly going round and round. We were in blood-sugar-deficit and perhaps our senses were impaired. We stopped and stood at the edge of the very high Bubbs Creek, scanning the far banks for the telltale orange of bear, or jack-squat, boxes. It's not like the Park Service, an arm of our federal steward of the land, Department of the Interior, to put obstacles like rivers between you and the boxes. But, at that moment that was what we knew they had done to us. Just to add to our day's hardship.

"Bridge must've been washed out by the storm," Chuck conjectured.

"Yeah, must've. No way to cross this."

But Chuck was already trying to walk across the creek that rushed up his thighs. He leaned steadily into his $200 adjustable walking sticks for security.

"Where you going?" I asked.

"Where's it look like I'm going?"

"Is that a rhetorical question?"

"Does it sound like one?"

Propelled by an old tape, girls can't do what boys do, I stepped in the white water to follow my big brother. "People die doing this every year," I said. The water was powerful and moving at least 50 mph, maybe 150 mph, for all I could gauge. Chuck turned around to retreat back up the bank. I turned to follow. Then, it happened really fast—Chuck slipped on a slimy rock and fell and was bathed up to his shoulders in the rushing water. And, somehow—the power of his suggestion?—I slipped too and got soaked up to my neck. We climbed to safe ground and watched in silence as both of his expensive walking sticks floated like toothpicks down the flume of furious white water, forever out of our sight. Somewhere in a reservoir of the Central Valley Project way on down in the fertile San Joaquin Valley would be their graveyard.

"Shit," we said in tandem, briefly united against a cruel force of nature.

"I fell . . . I was trying to grab your sticks," I said, shaking the water out of my deep pockets."

"Yeah . . . why didn't you grab them. I was trying to hand them . . . to help you," he said sloshing away from the creek.

"Why'd you throw them in?"

"I didn't throw them in . . . I was trying to give you one to hold on to." To this day his version of the story goes, "Yeah, I was trying to save my sister from drowning in this raging river when I lost these sticks . . best walking sticks I ever had." Oh, the revisionist history.

"Where could those bear boxes be?" I said.

"Let's skip it—we'll just hang the food or something."

" . . . Fine with me."

We changed into dry clothes, set up the tent, made camp, and cooked our dinner, some dried concoction that was worth its weight more for warmth and ritual than for gustatory delight. It was a gorgeous, lush meadow and the charm of the trip was restored briefly by the singing of Bubbs Creek.

Chuck was sprawled out on his cushy ground pad—a full-length one. Mine was a skimpier three-quarters length. I'm sure we had argued, somewhere along the line, about the merits and demerits of both.

"Well at least we're clean," I said.

"Yeah, and it doesn't look like rain tonight."

We were sated enough to count blessings. And to ignore the 900-pound gorilla: where to stash our food for the night? There were no proper trees for doing the counter-balance hanging system. They were tall, but their limbs didn't extend far enough from their trunks.

We had heard that wedging it between boulders sometimes works. So like little kids hiding contraband goods from their parents, we found a haunch of granite with a deep crevice that we imagined, in our deluded state, to be the most clandestine slot in the forest.

We ceremoniously wrapped and wedged between granite boulders our remaining food, which included our breakfast, my precious coffee, and our energy food for the long (14 miles) hike out. We mustered enough energy to carry two heavy flat boulders to put on top of the wedged food. Together they probably weighed about 100 pounds. We placed our metal cooking pots on top of all, the standard forest alarm system, on the off chance that a bear might try to get our food as we soundly slept.

Exhausted, we climbed into our sleeping bags.

"I'm going to sleep like a lead balloon," one of us, probably me, must have said.

"I'm gonna sleep like a dead door nail," the other must've reported back.

But again that gurgling creek, which I have since decided is haunted, power-tossed rocks and boulders and tyrannized me with a dozen auditory hallucinations from marching bands to angry crowds to cattle stampedes to Beethoven's Ninth. At one point it mimicked a chorus of shrill voices crying, *The bear! The bear!*

Sleep came at brief intermissions. I dreamed I was back in our family home on Price Street in Rahway, New Jersey. I was running up dark stairs away from some scary presence in the cellar. I dreamed my mother was percolating coffee and I smelled the aroma and heard the ping of the aluminum pot with the glass bubble top. I heard the aluminum pans again hitting rock. I turned over, knowing my mother was near and all was right. Something was out there, I knew in my shallow sleep, but couldn't we just sleep through it? Hadn't we slept through loud parties, our brother's rock 'n' roll band, the explosions at Esso refinery and at the local chemical factories? My mother banged the pot really hard.

And my brother, whose survival skills were honed in jungled places far more treacherous than the forest, sounded a reveille.

Bears! Get up!

I jumped up, my heart racing like an engine whose idle needs resetting. It was 2 a.m. and very dark with no moon. Stars salted the sky and we could barely make out the tall Jeffrey and Ponderosa trees around us. We stood 10 feet from where the food was. Chuck shone his light. It was not *a* bear. Six golden yellow eyes bored holes in the night. We could decipher two cubs and the mother nearby, apparently prompting her kids.

"Oh, my God," I repeated, "the mother is preparing them for a life of crime. Stealing human food!"

We both yelled to them to get out of there. But it was clear the cubs had a mission this night, sanctioned by an adult. I blew my whistle. We made enough of a racket to wake our dead grandparents in New Jersey. The rangers say this works. The rangers say lots of things. And my brother listens to them. But those three bears stood their ground. "You want us to do what?" they seemed to mock us.

Chuck, ever dutiful to authority, moved toward the food to get it away. "We are not allowed to let the bears have it," he said as if he were about to take his toy back from a child.

"Are you crazy? Chuck, let the bears have the food," I yelled.

"What about your coffee?" he said.

"Chuck, get the food. Quick!"

What took us 45 minutes to set up, the beasts had undone in seconds, with the swipe of a talon. The bears, at least having a healthy dose of shyness, kept at bay as Chuck edged in and grabbed the food. Which was crazy. Bears are dangerous, especially cubs-cum-mama. But my brother Chuck was no stranger to danger. He had been in war zones, including Santo Domingo and Vietnam, and, even more scary, he had graduated from Dad's Boot Camp.

The food bag was a mess, torn up by the bears who also slobbered over it. I'm here to tell you that a bear's incisors cut through nylon and Ziploc plastic bags like a hot needle through wax. "We have to destroy this food or we'll never get rid of them," said Chuck.

Right.

"Let's throw it into the river so the bears won't get it either and be done with it."

Right.

"The coffee, too."

Wrong.

"I have to keep a little bit of coffee for my last morning," I said stupidly. I knew it was stupid as soon as it was out of my mouth.

"You can't, they'll smell it and just keep coming back."

"I'll get a bad headache if I don't have my Peet's Sierra Dorada blend," I whined.

But it wasn't only the physical discomfort. My strong morning coffee, I reasoned, was my only vice. It wasn't just the pharmacological effect of caffeine. It was the brewing, the blossoming aroma, the first sip, during which I ritualistically made noise as I sucked in the proper mixture of air to open my taste and olfactory apparatus to Mother Nature's very own design for getting one chemically balanced to seize the day. It was my carpe diem. It was the very beverage our own mother, as maternal as the cubs' mama, gave us in a bowl with hot milk at a very young age. The beverage that loosened our tongues, my five sisters and mine. How could I face the day without its soul-stirring energy? How could this guy be my brother and even suggest such a travesty? Oh what anguish.

While Chuck was throwing food systematically into a deep part of the creek, I fiddled around with my stuff and my sacred grounds. "OK, here goes the coffee," I said, casting the wad into the creek. Gone, washed away. I made the sign of the cross.

For the second time in three years, at Junction Meadow, we had to hurry and break camp in the dead of night, this time while three bears watched our every move. As we hiked with our headlamps on, a thin moon cast some light through the trees and shone on something off to our left, not many paces from our site. Even in the dark, I detected its industrial orange paint. It was the oblong metal food storage box we had failed to find. If bears have any reasoning power, they must've wondered about ours. We went a good mile under starry heavens and found a spot of soft duff where we simply laid out our sleeping bags to catch a few hours of sleep.

"I smell coffee," said Chuck when we were settled.

"What do you expect—it's all over my hands from handling it," I said. "Don't worry."

We fell out quickly but were up early and without breakfast tramped the last 14 miles back to Cedar Grove. I offered to share one of my walking sticks with Chuck, but he refused. My caffeine-withdrawal headache pulsed along with the bunions on my hip bones and spurs on my trapezius muscles. It was a beautiful sunny day, but thanks to the rain and thunderstorms that spurred us on earlier in the trip, we had covered the trail a day faster than the first time. (I have since come to believe in the "Chuck Factor"—when out with him, one needs only the slightest provocation to cover ground more quickly. But that's another story.)

I was staying the night at the Cedar Grove Lodge in Kings Canyon, so I told Chuck to take a shower there if he wanted to before the five-hour drive home to Los Angeles. But once out of the woods he is always eager to get in his car and hurry home to his wife.

"No thanks," he said, "I'll just call Cheri and have her get the hot tub ready for me."

"Sounds great," I said refraining from my usual dig about his L.A lifestyle. We walked to his car and agreed it was another good trip, notwithstanding the bear incident.

He shuffled around in the parking lot and beamed, "You know, you can't really appreciate simple things like pavement til you've done this type of trip."

"Yeah," I beamed back. "You're right about that." I marched my overused feet in place "Flat pavement. Feels great. The things you miss in the backcountry . . ."

"Yeah," he said. "Another great trip."

"Wonderful. Wait til Cheri hears the bear story."

"Whose version?"

"Aw, g'head, you tell her yours."

We hugged and he was gone. And I couldn't wait to get out my stash and make my Sierra Dorada. I'd saved just enough and it would be richly rewarding and uncommonly smooth, to borrow the TV marketing pitch from a vice I don't have.

I heated up some hot water with my camp stove, brewed it, noisily took my first sip—ahhhhhh—and sat down with a local paper. I read with great interest a story about a man leading a Sierra Club trip a week earlier on the same trail we had just followed. He was mauled by a bear. Apparently, he had taken his food into his tent with him at night after a bear came snooping. The bear returned and reached into the tent hoping to abscond with the food and swiped the man's scalp in the process, bad enough to call for an emergency exit from the wilderness.

Imagine that. I just sipped my joe and shook my head. Never, ever fight with the bear. That much even I knew.

6

Curing Cheri in Big Sur, 1997

I watched Chuck's wife, Cheri, take the cure along Big Sur's Pine Ridge Trail. It was my sister-in-law's first and last backpack trip. It was the kind by which we now count the years, that one being known as "the summer Cheri went to Big Sur . . ."

For all the times Chuck and I have backpacked into the wilderness, Cheri, has never expressed any hankering to join us. Not once.

"Her idea of roughing it," says Chuck, "is when the towels at the Ritz Carlton have not been changed." Still, it was Chuck who wanted Cheri to experience an activity that for him is always momentous (I have not pointed out to Chuck that Cheri, who had only two siblings, does not share our childhood trauma of long waits for the bathroom. Call me Ms. Freud, but I still think it's the instant access to the ubiquitous john that sealed our addiction to backcountry trips. I can support this hunch with a telling statistic: A recent survey revealed that my siblings and I collectively own, or rent, 30 bathrooms; that's three per capita. I don't know what the American norm is, but I'm sure we are higher.)

Chuck and Cheri go back 36 years to their freshman year at Rahway High School. They met at a dance. Their meeting was very much like the scene in Westside Story where Tony and Maria met—the room became silent and everyone, the band and all stopped and they saw only each other. Chuck sang a song called *Cheri* (it's pronounced with the accent on the second syllable, like Marie), which he made up on the spot. O.K., I'm making this up. I have no idea how they first met, but I'm sure if I asked it would be a similar scenario, from Cheri's perspective. Chuck would probably say something like he helped her with her math homework (big prevarication!).

I do know this is true: Chuck invited Cheri to dinner and told her he was an only child. When she arrived, she asked *Who are all these people?* the answer being obvious. "I didn't think you would come if I told you I have nine brothers and sisters," he said.

Cheri has gone through many momentous events in Chuck's and my family's life, including being there when Chuck joined the Army, when he left for Vietnam, and when he returned from the war after being injured as a paratrooper jumping from the plane.

Cheri has known me, Chuck's younger sister by five years, through my many incarnations from good Catholic schoolgirl, rabid Beatle fan, and hippie to aspiring Barbizon model, born-again feminist, and card-carrying Zen Buddhist—and wilderness lover.

In her sometimes eye-rolling acceptance of all these phases, Cheri is more like a sibling than an in-law. She has shared in historic turning points in my life—she took Grace and me to see our first of 12 screenings of the Beatles' film, *Hard Day's Night*, and was there when I graduated from Beatlemania to real boys. She was the one who told me I was skinny enough to be a model—which sent me to Barbizon. She was present for many rites of passage in my family, including one episodic day more than two-and-a-half decades ago when my father, after waving a pistol in a drunken state, gave up alcohol.

Although she and I have chosen such diametrically opposed paths in life (she's built her life around her husband and kids, I've built mine around career and freedom to travel), we have much to share in my long, sometimes very animated, family history.

Cheri marvels at how Chuck drops his corporate persona and becomes a regular backwoods guy for some time before and after our outdoor forays. When things are especially stressful at his corporate job, as they often are, Cheri calls and tells me so through the code phrase, "He needs a weekend in the woods." She has been more than content to live each trip he takes through the opportunistic caterpillar, stray duff, and woodsmoke that invariably hitchhike home on Chuck's gear.

She listens raptly to Chuck's version of the bear encounter, the river crossing, the arguments we had over my coffee fetish, his gear fetish. Then she calls me and gets my version and I tell her no, he didn't save me from the bear or from falling in the river. It was the other way around. I tell her no, it's not my freshly ground Peet's coffee that weighs so much, it's his water filter, global positioning gadget, camera, and binoculars. He tells her how I'm going to get giardia one of these days because I drink from mountain streams. I tell her his dutiful filtering

91

of pristine snowmelt is overkill, a product of corporate America's idea of hygiene. She is thoroughly entertained by both versions of events and perceives that our banter is all part of the routine we await each summer with the anticipation of soldiers being granted liberty.

Although for Chuck—and for me, too—our retreats into the woods have had the quality of divine revelation, it has been hard for Chuck not having his wife share in the pleasures along the trail. For me it doesn't matter if my partner shares all my passions. So I have never completely understood why that summer weekend, July 4, Chuck got Cheri to agree to having a go at this activity that transforms him into a paragon of serenity.

My boyfriend, Dan, and I drove down from San Francisco and Chuck and Cheri drove up from Los Angeles. We met at the Pine Ridge Trail. The trail starts from the stunning, bluff-jumbled Big Sur coast and was as good a choice as any for Cheri's first (and last) trek.

Along this popular and well-traveled trail, she would have lots of company as we traversed redwood-shaded glens and fern-filled gullies, held our ear to the roar of Big Sur River's cascades, gazed across a canyon to chaparral-mantled Mount Manuel, or admired the skeletal outcroppings bulging from the chunky Rubenesque Santa Lucias. Come to think of it, there was every reason Cheri should have been a convert to sleeping in the great outdoors.

The winter had been a very wet one with great inundations of rainfall, so backcountry river and stream beds were refreshingly swollen. And the plum of this particular trip was Sykes Hot Springs, hot water oozing from profound cracks in the earth. The springs were tucked a deep, winding 12 miles into the Ventana Wilderness. All of this certainly would distract our novice hiker from her labor up and down the trail's unrelentingly steep grades.

I knew we were in trouble the first mile when Cheri said, "So, this is what you do all day, just walk?" If I were left speechless by her question she never knew it and what I said surely sounded like a bunch of non-sequiturs. I pointed to lingering wild iris on the side of the trail, to the carpet of redwood sorrel creeping under its eponymous tree, to a surprise pile of coral-tinged flicker feathers. How lucky we were, I exclaimed to her, to spot yellow and red columbine and a fairy lantern in midsummer. But as we traversed an open marble-stone slope I glanced back at Cheri. She wiped sweat with a bandana and I could tell that all that loomed for her were the intense dry heat, the hot spots on her feet, her sore shoulders, and tight calves.

A California writer, Rebecca Solnit, has written a tome called *Wanderlust: A History of Walking*. She calls the act "the most obvious and the most obscure thing in the world, this walking that wanders so readily into religion, philosophy, landscape, urban policy, anatomy, allegory, and heartbreak." The ability to walk over long distances on two legs, unique to our species, has generated some of our most creative poetic, meditative, and philosophical work, Solnit notes, from "the English romantic poets to the footloose Chinese and Japanese poets to the ruminating Henry David Thoreau and Walt Whitman."

Yes, all we do all day is walk.

"Walking, ideally," Solnit writes, "is a state in which the mind, the body, and the world are aligned, as though they were three characters finally in conversation together." I knew that some discourse wood assuage and distract Cheri, but I myself was one of those three characters, Solnit's "three notes suddenly making a chord." How often are we permitted to do free-range thinking? Why on earth would we do anything but walk—and think? I didn't pose these questions to Cheri, who looked pretty miserable.

Seven miles out, at Barlow Flat, we pitched our tents on the beach beside the Big Sur River. A refreshing mix of hardwood trees—tanbark oaks, bays, maples, alders, sycamores—stood behind us. The gently flowing river beckoned. And after several soaks in the river's green-tinted swimming holes, Cheri was talking to Chuck again. But Chuck was annoyed. Some neighboring campers were skinny dipping in one of the deep pools. This was not what he brought his wife to see. Dan and I shook our heads and laughed. We were after all in Big Sur, ground long trod by naturists of one sort or another, from the Esselen Indians to the bohemians of Henry Miller's day and the hippies since the 1960s.

The next morning, we took only day packs to make the hike the three miles farther to the legendary Sykes Hot

Springs. Reaching the place along the Big Sur River where the springs bubble up, we had to choose between a boulder-hop or calf-deep wading over the final half-mile to the hot springs. Cheri chose the boulder hop and we all followed, hopping, hoping—wishing—she could enjoy this as much as we were.

The springs are as funky as any tub would be that is constructed along dirt banks with burlaps sandbags the color of a teen boy's T-shirt after he's skate boarded on his back for half a day. The dun-colored bags, looking old and historic at best, section the 100°F springs into several stone-lined basins. And let's not forget the requisite naked people strolling through the woods, who looked as you might expect, like hippies, aged ones and neophytes. Cheri cast an indifferent eye, but of course Chuck disapproved.

We sank into a warm spring with naked people, who smiled welcomingly. All the mystique of Sykes has to do with a realtor's favorite mantra—location. The remote gushing waters are warm and draw bathers mainly because they are deep in this natural temple, the Ventana Wilderness. Everyone except for us was bathing nude.

One of the nude bathers sharing our tub, a young man, said to Cheri, "How about a foot massage?" I saw shades of the corporate disapproval that he usually checked at the trailhead cloud my brother's face as his wife floated her swollen feet, one at a time, into the hands of the stranger. She took her cure with great gusto. Pine Ridge was, after all, her first—and last—backpack trip.

7

Sister Act, 2000

How did a nice Sicilian Catholic girl like me end up deeply immersed in Zen Buddhism? These days there seems to be a certain cachet to claiming to be Buddhist but in 1988 when I joined the San Francisco Zen Center its halls were as lively as a ghost town. There had been a scandal—the usual: teacher sleeping with student(s), mismanaging funds—and the congregation or *sangha,* had fled the monastery under a cloud of disillusionment and righteous indignation. But I, on the other hand, an opportunistic passer-by who was long ago cured of blind faith in any one god, guru, or dogma, needed a place to live temporarily. The temple was so empty that I was given a stunning room with a view of a classical courtyard for a ridiculously low sum. Today that room is available only to senior priests and abbots.

No one ever forgets the first time they walk through those heavy wooden doors of the landmark Julia Morgan building into the resoundingly silent halls of the Zen Center. The swish of black garments might be the only sound if there is a retreat going on. The day I set foot into what is called Beginner's Mind Temple, I was met by a priest, Paul Haller. We sat on the grassy scented tatami mats in the Buddha Hall, flooded by fog-tempered light, behind us a gorgeous altar of compassion with fresh colorful flowers, sandalwood incense, and a medieval stone Buddha (the Awakened One). Wrathful gods were at each of his sides, as was a gilded Avalokiteshvara (aka Quan Yin).

I told Paul that I came from a big Sicilian family. I didn't think this sitting still was compatible with my inbred nature. We people move a lot, our bodies, arms, hands, and all. We express ourselves through motion. We're kind of organically wild souls, I don't know about this sitting still stuff. Don't know. Paul sat cross-legged, ramrod straight, smiling, listening. Then he told me that he came from Ireland from a big Irish Catholic family of nine kids. He was very dedicated to the practice of "just sitting." I relaxed and settled down. Hot damn, Sicilians welcome.

OK, I gave it a try. I sat in half lotus, tush on the cush, eyes gazing at a 45-degree angle, hands in the mudra (left palm resting on right, thumbs just touching). My first sitting of forty minutes went so well, I patted myself on the back, only to soon learn all meditations are not so calming.

The stillness of the body (not always of the mind), sitting on a cushion, focusing on a blank white wall with the Self in the form of thoughts and emotions coming with the speed of light, was a novel experience. The stillness set up a container, a framework to hold everything in place, from the resentment I felt toward the man who had just forced me out of my apartment (a sordid story not worth repeating) to the cosmological constant of anxiety inherited from my father and maybe his forebears. Most therapies worth their pricy therapeutic hour help you, if you are mostly on the sane end of the bell curve, to mediate the boundary between your inner and outer realities. Likewise this practice. Here was a bargain therapy with the guidance of many teachers who were all committed to "study the self to forget the self" by "turning the lamp inward."

The onion metaphor of Self as an entity of many layers that we peel away has always seemed apt. (Sometimes, the metaphor of lifting veil after veil fits better.) Eventually I believed that the so-called core itself is just another layer, shifting, dynamic, never fixed.

Nothing, absolutely nothing, is solid.

The first message I got from the Zen Center was *you already know everything you need to know* and *you are perfect the way you are.* Later I heard, *and you could use a little improvement.* The emphasis on loving kindness (*metta sutta*) and compassion overlapped with my Catholic training but the idea that we are all *One*, not separate, was new and still requires that I cleanse my doors of perception to feel it deeply. The emphasis on wisdom, symbolized by a swipe of Manjusri's sword cutting through delusion, stresses that Zen is experiential.

As I read the works of Zen teachers—Suzuki Roshi, Robert Aitken, Reb Anderson, Charlotte Joko Beck, Sylvia Boorstein—I felt I had been born with a "way seeking" mind always meant, Sicilian genes or not, to embrace Zen. A central concept of Buddhism, *shunyata,* translated as *form is emptiness* or as *inter-being,* has spawned tomes and tomes of explicating writings. This concept that ultimately says there is nothing solid in the world is paradoxically what I feel most grounded in. If nothing is solid—and more and more even science proves that— then even suffering is an illusion. Granted it takes rigorous focus to deconstruct the truth of that. (You'll have to experience that truth for yourself.)

My big family is a microcosm of the Buddhist concept of *shunyata*, or inter-dependent co-arising. Despite the fact of certificates recording successive years of our births, in the grand scheme we arise and fall as a unit. As does the entire human race. As you ponder that, come again to Sicily with Grace and me.

I have loved connecting deeply with my Sicilian roots through many visits to the old country over the past twenty-four years and it remains one of my abiding spiritual quests. For one trip to the island, I considered the novelty of sleeping in monasteries and convents— Italy's monastic bed-and-board tradition harking back to medieval times. As a devoutly lapsed Catholic, I still relish pealing bells, glowing candles, and incense. In fact, perverse as it sounds, I was, once again for a spell living in a monastery, the San Francisco Zen Center.

When Grace heard I was going, she piped up, "Ooohhh, can I go?"

My first thought was, "Just like old times, younger sister wants to tag along." Until about 30 years ago, we were two peas in a pod. Then she went the mortgage-marriage-kids route and I went off in search of the metaphysical.

"Let me think on it . . . ," I answered, remembering how we were once arrested for trespassing on an old freighter in Secaucus. Miraculously, our parents never found out. And once at Mother Seton Regional all girls' Catholic high school we were called down to the principal's office along with Chris and Kathy, co-conspirators in The Groupe. Sister Ignatius accused us of using "mafia tactics." True, we had, all four of us, gathered around the new girl, who came in from Jersey City and was dissing MSR as inferior to her last school. We had verbally thrashed and threatened her (to do what, I don't know). OK, it was a little "gang-landish" but *mafia?*—wasn't sister leaning a little on ethnic slur? We made friends with the new girl (who a few years later when I was waitressing in a diner came and left me a big tip).

Before we gravitated toward being bad and rebellious, Grace and I both won first place medals in religion bees in grammar school—all of which is to say we started out devout and could ace memorization of the Baltimore Catechism (to this day).

"Of course," I answered Grace. "Get on board."

We had invitations from two other siblings, Terry and her family and Tom and his family, (who by pure coincidence were visiting Sicily this year) to stay in their rented beach-side villas in the relatively modern resort, San Vito Lo Capo, west of Palermo.

"Too predictable," I told Grace. "We need places with curiosities—like Grandma's cedar-scented attic—with mystery and magic."

"I'm with you," she said, entrusting me, as always, to plan her first-ever journey abroad. *Buono*. With that I faxed off reservations, looking forward to worldly days of touring, reverent evenings in the quietude of hermitages.

We flew into Palermo and enjoyed an inaugural feast of pasta with fresh sardines and chickpea-flour frittata (*panella*), before taking to the madness of driving that frenetic city in our rental car. Fortunately, our first morning was on the serene bright hilltop refuge of the Sisters of Bell'amore. The sun blazed through our bedroom like a shaft of grace from heaven. Grace remained sound asleep, just as she used to back when I would get up and go to mass before school. Alone, I joined the Sisters of Beautiful Love in the subterranean chapel and did something I hadn't done in years.

"I received Holy Communion," I confessed to Grace over carafes of steamed milk and espresso.

"We're going to Hell anyway," she said, still shaking sleep.

"So are the clergy here," I told her. "The priest and nuns giggled during the Mass. Father fumbled the liturgy. Is nothing sacred?" I postured.

"My morning sleep…and our next cappuccino," she yawned.

And so we inaugurated our routine as each monastery reinforced the established rhythm of our lives. I'd be up

101

early each morning (the universal hour of mysticism) holding a figurative magnifying glass up to anything in the monastic setting—a Renaissance fresco, an old white-bearded man who never left the church pew; a marble altar with a huge wooden choir and 500-year-old pipe organ; the archetypal friar who strolled the halls with a ring of skeleton keys hanging from his triple-knotted cord.

Throughout our drives around the island, I told Grace I had something important to show her: the cult of the Great Mother. I had been reading a lot about Sicilian antiquities, including fellow Sicilian and writer Marguerite Rigoglioso's work on the Virgin Mother of the Mediterranean—goddesses or "creators who birthed the entire cosmos without need of a male consort." Marguerite explores "evidence of the original parthenogenetic power of deities such as Athena, Hera, Artemis, Gaia, Demeter, Persephone, and the Gnostic Sophia." Marguerite's life work is devoted to researching the *Cult of Divine Birth in Ancient Greece*, which includes Sicily, part and parcel of Magna Graecia. I have admired Marguerite's devotion to what is viewed as a cult. Her mother died suddenly when she was only ten and the tragedy thrust her into her life's work and meaning. She writes of her "death initiation into Persephone's mysteries" in a blog piece saying, "My mother's death serves as the blueprint of my identity, the seed of all subsequent fruits I have continued to bear. It is my curse, my cross, and my most holy blessing. That terrible death bite was a kiss of sweet nectar, without which I would not have been nourished these many years. It is what has propelled me forward, under, up, over, and down and back again."

It may seem ironic that I share something—the quest after the sacred feminine—with Marguerite who was left motherless at a tender age while I still have a mother figure into ripe age. My living mother has many good and loving qualities. But Grace and I have never felt a strong connection to our mother, only a sort of respect and familial devotion. It's not enough.

Our quest began in Erice, on the west end of the island. Driving up Monte Erice on the serpentine road that ascends steeply from the drab streets of seaside Trapani, we could see the prime real estate that attracted the Elymians, who settled here before the Greeks. As we rose, sweeping views took in Trapani's sickle-shaped coastline and its salt marshes, and the misty humps of the Egadi Islands scattered offshore.

The village of Erice is dominated by the crenelated turrets and tower of Castello di Venere, a crumbling 12th century Saracen and Norman castle built over a temple to Aphrodite (Venus to the Romans). The castle ruins embrace the remains of Roman baths and a dungeon. There's nothing to see of the temple, where a cult of priestesses personified Venus in the flesh—"sacred prostitutes" who assisted mortals hoping to sire divine offspring.

The Mediterranean peoples' worship of the goddess of fertility, whether of Astarte (Carthaginian), Aphrodite (Greek) or Venus (Roman), was entrenched in Erice for

1,000 years before Christ. Over the centuries the church channeled devotion to the goddess into devotion to the Virgin Mary. Yet up to modern times, Erice has been known to celebrate Aphrodite in spring with processional fanfare. While you can't see the ancient sites you can feel that goddess devotion in the air, a parallel universe. Grace has supernumerary powers and Feng Shui training that let her sense the metaphysical and see beyond the eye's range.

I told her there is something else about mystical Erice that has always intrigued me. Robert Graves, classical creator of I Claudius, writes in the preface to his novel, Homer's Daughter, how *The Odyssey*, was more likely written by a woman, a Sicilian, living near Erice. I told Grace all about this, how Graves writes that *The Odyssey*, "was composed at least a hundred and fifty years later than *The Iliad* and how it is "sweeter, more humorous, more civilized . . . a poem about and for women." What with "Penelope living riotously with fifty lovers." Graves says that, "Apollodorous, the leading classical authority on Greek myths, records a tradition that the real scene of the poem was the Sicilian seaboard, and in 1896 Samuel Butler, the author of Erewhon, came independently to the same conclusion. He suggested that the poem, as we now have it, was composed at Drepanum, the modern Trapani, in Western Sicily [a shout away from Erice]." Graves finds all this evidence "for a female authorship irrefutable."

Grace, indulging my penchant for the mystical, stood reverently with me on the grass above the temple site. The feminine energy was palpable in this corner of ancient Sicula. Viva Aphrodite. At last Grace declared cappuccino time. And, feeling certain that Graves, Butler, and Apollodorus—and Marguerite—were right, I was ready, too.

Erice is the home of an earthly goddess of goodness, Maria Grammatico, a celebrated baker and master of the craft of painting marzipan, that sweet almond dough, to resemble fruit. Walking toward her shop on Via Vittorio Emanuele, we wound through Erice's narrow cobblestone streets, admiring flower-filled courtyards. The medieval mood holds up well if you don't catch a glimpse of the communications towers that lace the town's skyline. Sicily's sumptuous food, like its architecture, is textured by its many conquerors, most notably the Arabs. They brought sugar to Europe in the 9th century, as well as a genius for recipes incorporating almonds, pistachios and dried fruit. To me, this has its highest expression in ambrosial cannoli, the crisp pastry shell filled with creamy ricotta cheese and bits of all of these sweetmeats, as well as chocolate.

Fortified with Maria's cannoli, we were ready for our lodgings in Casa del Sorriso (House of the Smile). A hermitage that housed Franciscan monks from 1573 until 1970, the inn rises grandly above a steep pine forest with dizzying views of the Tyrrhenian Sea. It retains its monastic feel with vaulted ceilings, a contemplative cloister and low arched doors that lead to small, Spartan rooms converted from monks' cells. Each was furnished with a twin bed, chair and reading lamp, and each had a tiny private bath. Dinner was simple and good—marinated scungilli (conch), caponata (an eggplant and olive mix), rigatoni with a spicy meat sauce and the sweet, juice-gorged loquats that burst forth all over Sicily.

We had built flexibility into our itinerary to avoid getting stoned on ruins. Siracusa, the queen of Sicily's archeology treasures, would be our major stop. I was looking forward to seeing Siracusa with Grace, not only for the Greek city's treasures, but also because it is the birthplace of Santa Lucia, who in our household loomed like a deceased godmother. It so happened that our paternal grandfather died suddenly on the feast of Santa Lucia, December 13. On that day, in his and Lucy's honor our parents always prepared whole wheat grains cooked like cereal served with milk, brown sugar, and cinnamon. It's called *cuccia*.

The road to Siracusa on the built-up east coast took us through an oppressive brown industrial haze. We were relieved to find the city, once surpassed in beauty only by Athens, washed clean by sea breezes. The original nucleus of the city is Ortygia where the Duomo (cathedral) exemplifies the revolving-door culture of Sicily. It began as a 5th century BC temple to Athena, was consecrated as a church in the 7th century, used as a mosque by the conquering Saracens soon after, reconsecrated and adorned with mosaics in the Middle Ages, ravaged by an earthquake in the 17th century and renovated in the Baroque style.

There is so much to see from so many eras that Siracusa can be quite distracting. One afternoon, exhausted, we dropped into chairs at a cafe on the seafront promenade in Ortygia. Right there even, next to us was the Fountain of Arethusa, a freshwater spring. We sipped our mineral water and read this about Arethusa: While splashing in a river in Greece, the water nymph sensed the river god looking at her with desire. Wanting no part of his advances, she fled to Siracusa, where the goddess Artemis turned her into a spring.

We thought of the story of St. Lucy that we grew up on: A Christian virgin of a noble family in Siracusa, she gouged out her eyes in martyrdom rather than submit to the lust of a pagan who had admired their celestial blue color. Whichever legend you prefer, pagan or Christian, you have to marvel that Sicily has kept both alive over the centuries and that all of its cultural heritage is still accessible. Ah, but now I sound just like my father.

But it's true—there are so many riches of antiquity to mine in this small island. Even our leisurely three-day tour of Sicily's north coast effortlessly exposed us to ancient sites. Scopello, for instance, a steeply notched beach in the rocky shore about 20 miles east of Erice, is adjacent to the Zingaro Nature Reserve. This stunning park contains caves, to which we easily hiked and in which 12,000-year-old human skeletons have been found. A few miles up the road is the beach resort town of San Vito lo Capo. We stopped there to visit with our sister and brother, Terry and Tom and their respective families who were staying in

107

spacious condos. They invited Grace and me to alter our monastic journey and stay amid their luxurious lodgings—with no curfews.

I don't recall who first used the term family-itis. I think it was Cheri, Chuck's wife, when she noticed the state of my itching and twitching to get away, far away from la familia (I made a beeline for the mountains then). This condition strikes at times. Who are these people? I was born into the wrong family. I want to be from a family of two, me and a brother with red hair called Peter. He and I get along like white on rice. I'm nothing like these people.

I believe this condition must strike all of my siblings at times even if they don't admit it.

Presently, much as I love the tribal rites with my big clan, I was on a spiritual search of sorts. My boisterous kinfolk did not figure in that quest. Needless to say, Grace was only too happy to accept the invitation.

I drove off alone and happily for the night to a Benedictine abbey that dated back to the 6th century. Benedictines taught two of my brothers, Jim and Sal at St. Benedict's Prep in Newark, NJ. St. Benedict, born in Sicily in 1526 of African slaves was a follower of the Franciscans and a very charitable guy. The old stone abbey had its hair-shirt aura of attraction but did not satisfy any curiosity and, I hate to admit it, but I wished Grace were there to share in some mischief. I heard the monks were chanting vespers and was warned I could not go. I crouched unseen at the chapel wall to watch, until I was disinvited. I was the wrong sex to set foot inside—just like old times.

Next day I drove back to San Vito lo Capo to share dinner that evening with the clan. At the nearby trattoria, Terry's husband Dan, who is a fisherman by way of breeding at the Jersey Shore, told me, "Get the pasta with fresh anchovies, these guys know their fish." I was thinking, "Humph, I know all about it, I'm the Sicilian, not you."

My mind went back to 1976, the year I was doing graduate studies in southern France. I traveled down the boot to Sicily and only by spending hours in the village municipal building did I find my father's first cousins. We have been in touch since then. Terry's husband is Jewish so I told him how we may actually have been Jewish way back when. Possibly our family name came from Guzman, along with the Moors who were run out of Spain during the Inquisition. (Our mother's maiden name, Catalano, surely came from Catalan.)

Dan, who is about as religiously Jewish as I am Catholic, agreed and noted how there is a tiny village called Cusumano in Sicily and way back when, before anti-Semitism struck in a nasty way, if you were Jewish, you took the name of the village where you lived. Feeling historical outrage, I thought, *if you were Jewish they should have named the village after you.* Well, I admit neither practice made sense.

The next day Terry and Dan left for home and Grace and I agreed to meet up with Tom and his family in our cousins' village, Cammarata, later this week. Taking the scenic coast road instead of the express autostrada (except to skirt Palermo), we drove east to Cefalù. Cefalù, with its Rocca, has a landmark crag that towers over the town and the shell of a temple to the goddess Diana that survives at the top of La Rocca. I let Grace talk me into a lunch stop and it was a marvelous feast on the terrace of Trattoria Galante: briny-sweet shrimp and tender calamari polished off with a bottle of chilled Corvo, Sicily's crisp white wine.

Grace invariably slept late and during her waking hours industriously kept score—of our food and espresso stops, shopping, and beach sitting. Back on the monastery trail again, she seemed to enjoy the solitude at each sanctuary until the Franciscan one in Gibilmanna, which is pitched quietly against a dark forest at 2,500 feet above the Mediterranean. A reserved padre had shown us to our room and then we never saw him again, not even at 9:30 p.m. when, upon our return from dinner in Cefalú, it took an unsettling 10 minutes of banging before a shadowy figure unbolted a door.

"This one is *too* laid back," she stated. "You sure this isn't some retro form of penance?"

"Oh, a minor disturbance," I cajoled.

"Easy for you to say," she said.

"O.K, O.K.," I conceded, "Shopping tomorrow and to the beach in Cefalú." Actually, shopping is a form of penance for me, so I sat on the beach while Grace made the medieval village merchants happy.

However, once my sister had a prolonged taste of Sicily's convivial lay world, she was in no hurry to go back to the men and women of the cloth. But I had yet to quell my curiosity, so we compromised. Between our final convent stays, we would sandwich a night in the lavish San Domenico in Taormina.

"Can you get us in there?" she asked.

"Hey, I'm the Pope," I told my younger sister." But you'll have to put on a dress," I said, proffering the absurd notion that this would be a hardship for her. She couldn't wait to wear the $300 red summer dress that was unsuitable for the eyes of celibacy. Grace took to the decadent five-star hotel like an acetic to a hair shirt. She proceeded to help the jewelers of Taormina toward an early retirement, stocking up on 18-karat gold.

The drive along the coast from Cefalù to Taormina took five or six hours. We made one extended stop at Santo Stefano di Camastra, a ceramics paradise, where Grace stocked up on vases, tiles and bowls. After that I switched to the autostrada, and our only stops were at service areas, which serve the best espresso drinks.

Taormina, the island's aristocratic jewel, sits on a hill above the Ionian Sea, with a view of Mt. Etna's smoking volcano to the west. It has been a favorite resort of the elites since Greek days, and is worth a splurge. I had booked a room for one night at Taormina's highest-rated hotel, the San Domenico Palace, at $250 worth every lira. Being a former monastery does not diminish the hotel's air of luxurious indolence–spacious rooms with huge baths, gardens for strolling, a lap pool with bar service—but medallions and frescoes of martyr saints still watch from above doorways. Dinner on the elegant outdoor terrace was superb, if formal. I longed for the antics I'd experienced with my parents at nearby Ristorante Da Lorenzo. The waiters all but kissed the ground we stood on when they learned my parents had ten children (and thirty grandchildren).

All of which did nothing to prepare Grace for our return to a clergy-run lodging. At Noto's Benedictine convent, we were in the midst of the nun's attire we had been raised with—only face and hands exposed from beneath layers of form-blunting habit.

"Sister Celeste has a sweet, beatific countenance," I pointed out.

"Most unusual for a mother superior," said Grace.

By and by, several sisters came to our room to make sure, "*Tutt'é bene.*" Each knock was preceded by the dark penguin form visible through our frosted glass door.

"*Sì,* all's well," I assured each, even as the next morning I instigated a comedy of errors. I pushed a switch I thought would light up a Madonna and Child painting over my bed. Not knowing I'd rung an emergency bell, I went for a walk. Grace, whose Italian is sketchy, awoke from her deep sleep to frantic banging on the door, which she opened, idly wondering aloud, *"Dové sta mia sorella* (where's my sister)?" Sister proceeded to search my bed sheets, then the bathroom with a bewildered Grace in tow. They were engaged in energetic hand language when I strolled back in the room.

Resigned to not stumbling upon anything magical or otherwise mystical, I told Grace "We better pay a quick visit to their sister Benedictine house." In Modica, in the ocher-stone nunnery of a sun-steeped countryside woven with Sicily's ancient vines, olive trees, and citrus orchards, we at last learned a secret.

Fellow Sicilian American Laura, a novitiate from Cincinnati, led us through sunlit courtyards and dark chapels, then said, "Let me show you what I was doing when you arrived." She unlocked the door to a room dominated by a large hospital-green contraption that looked like an X-ray machine fitted with turntables. Marina, a fledgling nun from Poland, would not let us photograph her as she fed the machine water and flour, mundane ingredients that came out as large disks of Holy Communion host. Embossed with the crucifix, they were placed into the jaws of another apparatus that cut them into bite-size wafers, falling by the hundreds into buckets, to feed the faithful masses.

Laura beamed proudly. Nothing short of demystifying the Blessed Trinity could have stunned us more than "robo-host."

When we left, I asked Grace, "Did you have any idea?"

"No," she said as we drifted down a winding, sun-gilded road. "I thought they came down from heaven."

You could say I had now satisfied my trip's quest. But as is often the case, other insights not sought arrived when Grace and I stopped in Cammarata for a few days. First we stayed with Toto and Stella who have four young children. They loaded us with food, not unlike our Big Night in Acireale. Then we stayed with the Tuzzolinos who were so excited when we explained that Tom and Patty with their four kids were coming to meet them. Preparations began. There would be a big feast at another Toto's (Sicily is a land of many Totos) restaurant when brother Tom arrived. Somehow the time of his arrival was lost in translation. He would not arrive in time for the feast at Toto's and meal times are sacrosanct so we had to eat anyway. We did so in near silence. Grace and I watched our cousins' faces drop to the ground and a pall of disappointment big enough to envelop the village descend upon us. We understood that our arrival sparked joy but the son's arrival was to be an international incident of major proportions. They seemed devastated. Fortunately, Tom arrived later that evening and although the feast was less elaborate, all was not lost. He went on to forge a long, enduring relationship with the Tuzzolinos that eventually led to our trans-Atlantic family reunion in 2006.

As for Grace and me, we smiled to ourselves thinking of one of the island's three defining corners, where hints of the sacred feminine that once reigned supreme were still rife in the air. *Viva Aphrodite.*

8

Faithful Couple Meets Grizzly Giant, 2002

It blows my mind sometimes to think that I have spent more than ten years with a man who does not dance.

I come from a dancing tribe. My parents, 1940s beat dancers, have scuffed up hundreds, maybe thousands, of polished wood floors in their lifetimes and still dance all the swing dances of their era—the Truckin, Peabody, Suzie Q, and more, at 80 and 82. All of their ten children danced before they walked—coaxed to shake diapered butts to music. My oldest brother was a rock musician whose band considered our house jam central. Music and dance through four generations filled our home.

So how could I end up happily with a man who can't hum the hit songs of my youth, and who just sits there when I'm bouncing off the wall to some catchy tune?

Wilderness is the answer. A big part of the answer, anyway.

One day in 1992, not long after Dan and I had just met, I took a bold step. I invited him to go on an assignment with me to southern Yosemite where I would be researching a story for the magazine I worked for, then called *Motorland*. In hindsight maybe I was looking for something that gave this two-left-feet guy some semblance of rhythm. He was in every other way a man of substance. I just needed an inkling of his *style*.

It had been a long hiatus for both of us since our last visits to Yosemite. We were going to the southern end, not the over-loved valley, to avoid the "thousands of tired, nerve-shaken, over-civilized people," John Muir had noted there in 1898. Wawona, at the southern entrance, is the historical heart of this national park.

We left on an unseasonably warm fall day, the drive through the Central Valley whetting our appetite for the outdoors. Curvy, sunbaked roads rocked us side to side as we slid dreamily through time-warped towns, Manteca, Oakhurst, Escalon, the Gold Rush hamlet of Groveland. Then, at Big Oak Flat entrance, the brisk mountain air stirred our anticipation.

Before heading down Highway 41 to Wawona, we decided to lunch at the grand and elegant 1927 stone and sugar pine Ahwahnee in Yosemite Valley. This way, we'd at least glimpse the granite formations, Half Dome and El Capitan that are the chief currency of majesty in this once true wildland.

Dan, generally reserved with superlatives, exclaimed about the beauty of Yosemite. He was sorry there was not much water this drought year in the falls—Yosemite, Bridalveil, and along the Mist Trail. He remembered coming here as a kid with his big family—he was the youngest of five. They didn't have money for expensive vacations—and all came into the world discussing politics the way my family members hit the ground dancing.

When Dan was growing up in the 1940s and '50s Yosemite was a place where families could just show up and find a spot to camp out and cook their food. The big thrill back then was gathering at night to watch the firefall over Glacier Point, a practice discontinued in the early 1970s. Today you need reservations for everything, even camping and if you go in summer, expect Grand Central Station and horrific traffic jams—not a wilderness experience.

This October, the crowds were not bad. We continued on to our first night's lodging, the Tenaya Lodge, in the village of Fish Camp just south of Yosemite's southern entrance. We passed the burn areas from a recent fire. Charred trees, blackened snags, and patches of bald soil jolted our pastoral reverie. But pioneer plants were already starting life cycles anew: shrubs such as ceonothus, manzanita, and bear clover sprouted from stumps as did black oak trees; the roots of lupines and native clovers were enriching the soil with nitrogen for the next round of plants in the natural succession, a course that would run about 100 years before a conifer forest fills our view again.

After checking into the Tenaya, it was late and close to dinner, but Dan insisted we go for a stroll in the nearby Mariposa Grove of big trees, the largest of three giant sequoia groves in Yosemite. (The other two are the Tuolumne and Merced Groves near Crane Flat Ranger Station.) As we browsed through the peaceful stands of *Sequoiadendron giganteum*, I noticed something about Dan for the first time, maybe: He was smiling and very focused on the trees and although we spoke of their majesty, it didn't seem to matter if I were there. He was having some intimate moments with the big trees, which struck me as curiously charming. He had heretofore seemed an all too serious lawyer at times.

We stopped and read an interpretive plaque. The Grizzly Giant, an estimated 300 tons of gnarled heft, is the most impressive of these monster trees. At 2,700 years old, it soars 209 feet with a trunk bulging to 28.4 feet in diameter. But it is dwarfed by the 290-foot Columbia Tree, the grove's tallest. We didn't need vital statistics to settle into the soothing presence of cinnamon-red bark everywhere. The city, we had left just this morning, seemed lifetimes ago.

We were pondering two trees growing together, when a filled tram trolley that takes tourists through the grove rolled by and the tour guide pointed near us and quipped, "Now here's a Faithful Couple—the tree, folks, not the people." Faithful Couple, the tree, is two sequoias whose trunks have bonded for life. Which was ironic because I didn't think I'd ever be faithful to someone couldn't two-step or waltz.

Dan and I, moved on, grapevining with the tram all the way up to the Mariposa Grove Museum, which holds a good deal of informative displays on the giant sequoia, area plants and animals, and local history. Nearby we found the Wawona Tunnel tree, which must have been a formidable sight to come upon in 1969 when it was toppled by tons of snow in its crown. No wonder Faithful Couple bonded—the trees have a shallow root system.

The evening, still warm, seemed more and more romantic. As we headed down grove, we talked of capturing the beauty around us on film. This led to a discussion that got heated enough to border on an argument. He held that photographers were no less artists than those who worked in oil paints or water colors, say. I begged to differ and held that photographers were more technicians, artful ones, granted. I pointed out that, with training, I could hope to point and shoot a camera at a redwood to good effect, but I knew that no amount of teaching could give me talent with oil on canvas.

He countered that the manipulation done in the dark room and through the development stages requires a creative spark. Anyone can learn to manipulate "science" in imaginative ways, but between one's fingers and the finished canvas, there was only an amorphous medium, a simple tool, and the art derived from the effective surprise, unquantifiable creativity, talent. This was true art, I fairly yelled. The indignant attorney voice came out and he said not only was the photographer an artist equal to the painter, but how outrageous to consider otherwise. It began to feel like that discussion *Is there a God?* with only subjective premises and conclusions and personal conviction. We soon dropped it and walked in silence. It was very dark with no moon but we read a pulse of alpenglow through the darkened pines as a good sign—for the morrow, if nothing else.

119

In the morning, we filled three quart water bottles and our day packs with some freshly made penne in pesto, antipasto, gorgonzola, and fresh baguette from the Tenaya's deli. We headed for the Chilnualna trailhead where we parked and climbed steeply toward Chilnualna Creek. I liked that we could walk for long stretches together in comfortable silence, a necessary condition for any social being with a physiological need for the reverie. No relationship is more mis-matched, in my book, than that of the chatterbox and the dreamer. I have wondered if Dan's and my shared need for contemplative time is tied to our birth order, both of us being fifth children, buried in the deck.

On the steep trail, we crossed a ridge of fiery-barked manzanita, then entered a forest of ponderosa pines and incense cedars. About four miles out, with an altitude gain of 2,000 feet, we came upon the creek's several-hundred-foot-high falls. The Chilnualna Falls was more like a big trickle this dry year but it pours down an impressive deep chute. Atop the falls, we looked up another tier to a 60-foot cascade. Pools of icy green water from that one filled granite depressions, big enough for us to bathe our overheated bodies alongside swimming trout. It was very sensual and since we were serving our senses, we struck out again and stuck our noses right into the cracked puzzle bark of *Pinus jeffreyi*, a Jeffrey pine. It was redolent of its distinguishing heavenly vanilla scent. We picked at the pineapple-size sugar pine cones, their rosy interiors nibbled by squirrels, and got the sugary resin all over our hands.

We were in great spirits by the time we finished our strenuous 14 miles and got back to our new lodging at the Wawona Hotel, a restored National Historic Landmark. The New England–style hotel's surrounding meadows, lawns, and the nearby forest hills lend a tranquil feeling. An old covered bridge—for foot, horse, and stagecoach traffic—crosses the south fork of the Merced River. Near the hotel is the Yosemite Pioneer History Center, with historic buildings, horse-drawn buggies, and stage rides. Wawona is a phonetic spelling of the Indian call to owls, which the Indians believed were guardian spirits of the big trees. Native Americans called the Wawona area *Pallahchun*, "a good place to stop." We called it home for two nights.

And if I'd been with another person, I'd have called it a place to dance.

Wawona has the spirit of a country town where they don't lock front doors. Each evening, after a day outdoors, we looked forward to a little porch-sitting before dinner. On a comfortable sofa next to strangers, we would sit and just listen to the older folks chatter about nothing of consequence: the weather, the kids, their tee time on the historic 9-hole golf course. And there was legendary pianist Tom Bopp embellishing their moods—and mine—with golden tunes of olden days. But here was the piano and the standards and pop tunes I was weaned on and my feet and hips were moving in place. There was not an official dance floor, but a couple could, if they had a little chutzpah, swing out a bit, and go a couple of rounds. How I longed to.

After three months of our acquaintance, I knew enough about Dan that he was not to be moved to dance no matter how good he felt after a glass of wine or a day in the woods. I had, of course, once or twice grabbed his hand and tried to move him, but it was like trying to move a giant redwood—he stood tall, stolid, and even majestic.

I had certainly had spins with bad dancers. I had, in fact, throughout my 20s and 30s forged—or avoided— bonds with a guy according to how he danced. *Bad* dancers are usually *bad* because they lose the tension at the point of connection with their partner, which is an indispensable non-verbal cue for the successful push-pull, fluid give-and-take of weight, and shared bodily surrender to the music. I divide dancers into *waves* and *particles*—the former blend in and disappear into the music; the latter digitalize the sound and never get out of the counting in their head. Dan was not a bad dancer—he didn't risk that— he was just a no-dancer.

I don't know how seriously I take metaphors for life, but there is undoubtedly a connection between physical and mental. So, I had to ask myself as I vibrated in place to Bopp's music, quelling all my twitching muscle fibers, *Can this last? Are we wave or particle?*

I noticed there was still no moon and the deep sky prickled with stars and I didn't know that an answer would come the next day.

I had finished up my research for my story in the Wawona area, so Dan wanted to return to the valley and head out on the popular Mist Trail. Sure, why not.

We climbed up the trail passing the pitiful trickle of the first falls, Vernal, then we continued up steeply along the precipitous carved rock staircase to Nevada Falls. The riverbed, usually gushing with a deep glass-green and dangerous, frothy river, was a dry jumble of exposed boulders. But you could hop the boulders and on this hot day go stand in a residual pool under Nevada Falls, which, though swift and refreshing, was a mere phantom of its usual mighty self. Even so, it required caution.

Dan, a pushover for moving water (hates baths, loves showers, loves to run along a beach with churning waves) stripped to his blue, red, and yellow trunks and slid into the pool under the falls. The waterfalls are so spectacular in spring when the crust of winter loosens its grip and the snowmelt begins to run off the mountains with great sound, fury, and diluvial madness. The water runs with the might of a vertical river and visitors come from all over the world to behold the gushing from the granite walls, to hear the thunder, and be baptized by the magical spray from many yards away.

The icy waters brought that smile to Dan that he had shared with the big trees a few days earlier and again he seemed to be having a private communing with nature. More skittish about cold water, I climbed on a warm boulder to watch. That's when I saw more than the grace and purity of gravity, more than the physics of a falls seeking its own level over a pare of bare fleshy shoulders.

I saw the tension between dance partners. Dan stepped onto a dance floor and entered another plane, the way I do when I dance to a song I love. I could see him pick his rhythm, and vice versa, it was classical with an ancient beat, as Ellington might say, "older than time mathematics." As he warmed up under the icy falls, I saw him rise up under the water ricocheting into crystals off his goose flesh. He smiled and swayed to the white noise of the chute. *He was dancing.* The whole park emptied out and gave the man the floor. And then I saw him disappear, a total immersion in the icy green water. First there was a blur of smiling teeth, pink flesh, then a rippling smear of his primary-colored trunks, then just the beat and song of the falls. At last, I knew. This guy knows how to surrender to the music.

Caked with dirt and permeated with the smell of sweet river water and spicy forest air, we arrived at the elegant Chateau du Sureau in Oakhurst, just 45 minutes from Yosemite's southern entrance. We drove through the black iron gates of the Mediterranean-style inn, with its rippled tile roof, slate turret, and shale studded white stucco. We would finish a milestone trip in high style—putting on the ritz, after a fashion. The inn's Austrian owner, Erna Kubin-Canin, whose love of Provence is obvious, met and greeted us warmly, dirt notwithstanding. She showed us our room and noted how Wolfgang Puck, the famous Los Angeles restaurateur, had just stayed there last week. We sipped the first of our elderberry-scented libations, an iced tea, in our room.

At nightfall, we followed the lighted path past a lighted fountain to the elegantly understated Elderberry House. A fluted glass of champagne, crimson with elderberry nectar, arrived on a pewter plate for each of us. Erna's mix of imagination, exuberance, refinement, and earthiness characterized the dining, an experience we had earned. We savored a grilled fillet of halibut with a red pepper pasta and black bean sauce, a scintillatingly clear tomato consommé semolina dumplings. Lamb medallions were dressed with pear and ginger-elderberry sauce and served with a bread timbale. Seasonal vegetables included a delicious braised cabbage. For the final glorious extravagance, we shared caramelized apple tart and chocolate mocha torte. We licked every last atom of bittersweet chocolate lattices across our plate, clinked our champagne glasses together, and both wondered the same question that night more than ten years ago. *What next?*

9

Sister Satori in Cuba, 2002

We have survived so much together, my five sisters and I—four brothers, two parents, fifty years combined of Catholic school. I suggested we make one of our sisters' trips to Cuba. But only Grace (number six), who lives in Hoboken, and Donna (number ten), from the East Village, could join me (number five from San Francisco). Fine comrades they would be, having the requisite sturdiness for a trip to this embargoed country, abandoned in the '90s by the Russians to shortages of food, energy, medicine, and, of course, toilet paper.

I arrived in Havana two days before my sisters and declared to an immigration officer my trip's purpose—to learn about the culture. In the taxi from the airport I relished the American rock my driver played. "Cherish the love we have," sang Kool and the Gang. It was the turn of the millennium, with my government about to wage a shameful globally destabilizing war. That the twentieth century was dubbed the *American Century* of music for its outstanding influence was a source of pride in which to take compensatory refuge. I don't know what it is about arriving in a foreign and exotic country and being so tickled by hearing familiar sounds. OK, bring on the salsa now, I thought. Soon enough it would come.

Through email correspondence I had procured our rooms in a *casa particular*, a private home. The taxi arrived at Havana's Vedado neighborhood where gracious old mansions with Moorish details, stone balconies, and Greek columns sadly crumble. Here I encountered my first glitch.

My would-be host Jose Antonio Guerrero had no reservation for me and never heard of Marilena Diaz, the name of the person who took my reservation. A near-disaster ended well. Amiable Jose called his neighbors who generously took me in. Delmis and Octavio lodged boarders from Europe and Latin America. They gave me a bed with one light bulb over it, a hot shower, and hospitality reminiscent of my old Sicilian relatives. Delmis was proud of her faded beauty, which was warm inside with worn heavy Spanish furniture. She proudly toured me around her home, pointing out her intricately embossed family china. It was stuff like a TV and a stereo that drew my attention, "luxuries" I almost didn't expect to see in a Cuban home.

Really, what did I know about Communism?

Soon as I could I headed out into the tropical air. I headed down La Rampa, a long famous avenue. I felt a sense of liveliness in the air and noticed the small dark bodegas and the honey-gold light and that there were no single-occupant cars. I passed a churro vendor making the air fragrant with warm sugar and noticed Cubans kissing and talking, old and young, and a drunken woman who was entertaining until someone led her away. A young man thought I was Brazilian and another man stopped to ask me "Is tomorrow a work day?"

127

"Not for me," I said, "I'm a tourist."

"Oh," he said and proceeded to ask a nearby policeman. Another policeman stopped me to ask what time it was. I held up my watch for him to see.

In the city center, I sat for coffee at a ceramic table in Hotel Inglaterra, engraved with an auspicious line from poet Antonio J. Ponte, *A few paces from you lives your love at the nearest table, although you don't know it.* Seeing no prospects to fit that promise, I walked again, down the fashionable Obispo Calle and passed an ensemble of bass, guitar, and maracas. I marveled at what I came to think of as the Caribbean smile—everyone had beautiful teeth—and going-nowhere hands on swaying hips.

Detouring back to the Vedado, I tried to cross the Malecon but couldn't figure out the traffic rules. A woman scantily clad in a purple dress grabbed my hand and wouldn't let go. She led me through the traffic, which stopped for us. Four pairs of gringo eyes stared at me solemnly from the seawall. It occurred to me that the purple-clad woman was a prostitute. I thanked her for her kindness.

I had dinner at the Gringo Viejo my first night. I loved the yucca with cumin and onion, black beans and rice, which I dressed with the vinegar proffered. I passed on a terrible dessert of red gelatin with fruit cocktail. The bill with tip was $15.

I slept for ten solid hours that first night in Havana.

In the morning, Delmis's Spanish, to my ear, was a roll call of vowel sounds. Was she holding onto

128

consonants for an anticipated shortage? Despite our staccato communication, she lavished my morning with a bottomless demitasse of the syrupy velvet of Cuban coffee, tangy squat bananas, and guava paste with artisanal cheese.

My second night in Havana was New Year's Eve and Delmis invited me to dine with the family, which included her son and white-haired father-in-law. The *pollo agrodolce* (sweet and sour chicken) was delicious. We had nougat candy and almond paste (a sort of marzipan) for dessert. I sat with the family watching TV, entranced by the music and dancing, motifs that would be in abundance everywhere we eventually went in Cuba.

At one point, the TV screen flashed pictures of men's heads with a caption that I understood to say "prisoners of Imperialism." Next, the Cuban flag filled the screen and music played and everyone in Delmis's home stood and hugged, saying *Feliz año*. I watched the TV as more propaganda came on, ostensibly about how well the revolution was working. At last, old Fidel appeared kissing little kids and picking them up.

My hosts seemed uninterested in discussing the revolution. I respected their cues and didn't push. But whenever I could, I tried to read a newspaper. An article in the *Daily Communist* on the anniversary of the revolution showed a photo of gaunt people with the caption, "91 percent of the *campesinos* had some form of malnutrition before 12/31/58."

The rhetoric and propaganda I could glean sounded no different in spirit than the campaign stumping and promises at home where the Evil Axis was the new bogie man. And there was President Bush's platitude, *America is open for business*, urging Americans to get over the horrific grief of the recent September 11 attacks and go shopping.

After two days, I excitedly returned to the airport to meet my sisters. Donna's suitcase betrayed a telltale bulge. She had packed four pairs of shoes. Hadn't I advised my sisters to pack simply, not showy, for travel in this underprivileged country? Alas, Donna, last born in our clan, had suffered its most severe shortages—space, shoes, serenity.

"I plan on doing a lot of walking," she offered, anticipating my usual interrogation.

Grace was decked in gold necklaces. "You're wearing so much jewelry," I scolded them both. Donna twirled her chunky Lucite bracelet with coral-colored bugs suspended in it and shot back, "I see you're still wearing your PF Flyers from '72—or is it '62?"

"Sauconys," I retorted. Not since my misguided days at Barbizon modeling school, have we ever again shared the same sartorial concerns.

We hugged, recognizing our own brand of sisterly affection. In stage whispers, Donna and Grace discussed how I was the perfect head-to-toe candidate for the Extreme Team on the TV show, *Makeover*. I laughed hard and recalled with glee the magical realism of our last sisters trip to a decadent tropic, New Orleans, where all six of us had unwittingly locked horns with a Voodoo priestess on Rampart Street.

Traveling with my sisters is always an adventure. At the helm of our sister ship, I, at their insistence, plan the trips. I line up ambitious itineraries. Then, when we meet, it becomes patently clear that I have left out little details: time for primping before the mirror, gawking at souvenirs, lounging on beaches—things I consider a waste of travel time. Still, despite an often playful tug-of-war, we find common ground and always end up united by some euphoric meal, outrageous incident, or dark fiasco—like the witchy woman in New Orleans who made us tingle all over.

Our first day together this January took us on a hot, hazy, and humid walk from the Vedado toward old Havana again, a good four miles. As we walked, we shed clothes and stopped talking, each of us silently taking in the massive structures that had once housed single families. Perhaps we were painfully reminded of our own over-populated childhood home. With mere shreds of integrity intact—stone balconies, Ionic columns—these neglected jewels rose three-and four-stories high with ornate detail. Shelter for who knew how many, they were circumscribed by clothes lines with laundry hanging from column to capitol, the last remnants of candy-colored paint chips feebly peeling.

When we reached the Malecon (no shady lady to cross us this time), we became animated again by the dramatic ocean views made famous in the film, *Buena Vista Social Club*. The emollient mist floated with each crashing wave over the sea wall and revived us. We snapped away at cultural icons.

Not surprisingly, sister chemistry reconfigured the path I had plotted for our first day together in Havana. Instead of ogling Che Guevara and Fidel Castro's bloodied fatigues at the Museo de la Revolucion and a nearby display of bullet-ridden rebel vehicles, we lingered where rum-based mojitos were in ready supply— Hemingway's haunts, El Bodeguita and El Floridita. I was glad at least that we saw Hemingway's bed at Ambos Mundos, where a guide told us Hemingway came 1932 to 1939 and always took that same room, where he wrote *For Whom the Bells Toll*. That room felt like one of the world's sacred holy grails for writers, though I can't say that Papa's mojo infused my muse.

I had wanted to show my sisters the barrio with a gutted F.W. Woolworth's, where Habaneros queued up to buy beans and rice from gunny sacks. There I had seen an ad in black and white with happy athletic people that read, "They are happy because they eat vegetable protein." I gathered that vegetable protein was used to stretch meat. I had entered that Woolworth's expecting some semblance of the old five-and-dime variety store but the spacious interior cases were excruciatingly bare. People lined up at a counter waiting to purchase beans that were measured on old-fashioned scales by uniformed clerks. Rum and shoes were also sold there.

132

But instead we took baby steps down the upscale Calle Obispo—where the "dollar economy" that taps tourists is prohibitive to Cubans. The street pulled my sisters straight to a crafts market where Grace could satisfy half her souvenir quota with mementos in wood, ceramic, and cloth.

"This is the same kitsch from Cape May to Rome," I fumed, thinking of the cigar factory tour we were missing. "Don't even think of buying that," I said pointing to a big-rumped ceramic caricature of a *mulata*.

My only bargaining chip was the toilet paper that I was wise enough to bring along. But it was still early in the journey; that ace up my sleeve would have to be played sagely.

"Here, have this and be quiet," said Donna, tossing me a tan crocheted sweater that she had just purchased. They addressed me as *El Líder* or *Jefe*, Fidel's revered titles. I didn't mind, if they would just abide by my regime.

And, at times, I admit, I was easily seduced away from the rigors of my agenda. Why not enjoy, in addition to stodgy monuments like the Capitolio, the relentless beat of salsa in Café Paris, Lluvia de Oro, and Plaza de la Catedral? It was fun to watch Grace, who seemed to exude the perfect cocktail of pheromones and perfume. Men pulled her on the floor—or pavement—to dance while a crowd formed around them. Then, Donna would lure us up a tiny stairwell to an artist's atelier where the work was worth seeing and the airy balcony offered us a respite from the heat and a perspective on the hordes below.

We were united in our desire to eat a good dinner. One night we hopped these comical motorized yellow and green egg-shaped chariots and took a scary joy ride to a distant barrio. We were acting on a tip to a dining spot in a private backyard where we were able to eat some fresh shellfish, a delicacy in which we knew that most Cubans couldn't indulge. Other nights we found restaurants where we could enjoy smoked pork, steak, and always the wonderful plantains. We didn't mind eating like the locals—chicken, beans, and rice, a menu that was usually tasty and satisfying.

After several nights in Havana, we headed southeast to Trinidad. I drove our rented Toyota and over Grace's vehement protests, stopped to let Fernando, the first of many strangers, ride in the passenger seat. Her logic was sound—he could have been a psychopath. But I knew that any tourist who gets behind the wheel in Cuba is ethically bound to pick up hitchhikers who amass all along the route.

"Look," I said to Grace more righteously than intended, "you have got to get over your privileged ways."

Silence ensued as Fernando slipped his cassette into the tape deck and we bounced along to Bob Marley's *Jammin'*. Until I smelled something suspicious.

"Hey!" I yelled into the rear view mirror where smoke curled from cigarettes.

"You have got to get over your California ways," said Grace as she and Donna puffed away. *"Incredibile!"* I looked for support to Fernando, who apparently believed that driving was a shared activity as he attempted to downshift and begged me to slow down.

"You're scaring the guy," said Grace on a smoky exhalation. True, I was passing every car on the road—a slow parade of Detroit's heyday and people-packed truck beds. But I was doing only sixty.

Fernando, perplexed by our sisterly banter, asked to alight in Cienfuegos. We continued on to Trinidad, a living museum of colonial architecture, where (need I say?) we did more café-sitting and market strolling than museum and monument visiting. We stayed in a Soviet block-style hotel right on the Caribbean (four miles from town) in Ancon. Naturally those sisters of mine wanted to fritter away precious time on warm white sands, in blue-green waters and nearly staged a coup against me. Perhaps this was the moment to point out their dwindling tp supply.

Fortunately, Trinidad has interesting men, which helped to coax my sisters out of long hours of sun worship.

Osvaldo was the first to be taken into our entourage. We acquired him on our drive from the hotel into town. Osvaldo did not know that nearly everyone in his village where some 300 *casa particulars* are available, had flagged us down to take theirs. As he got into our backseat, he asked quietly, "Would you like a nice room?" Our synchronized reply, cumulatively the equivalent of *We don't want no stinking casa particular,* caused Osvaldo to

135

retreat instantly. "OK, sorry, sorry," he said in the most adorable sandpaper whisper. We bonded with him instantly.

Later that day, at the café El Meson del Regidor, we fell in love with Israel Moreno, acoustic guitar player, when he sang *Imagine* and *El Condor Pasa*. By evening, with men in tow, my sisters—and I, their witting accomplice—were colonizing the handsome traffic-free Plaza Mayor of Trinidad. Cubans and tourists alike were drawn to the spontaneous revelry. Without ever having had a lesson, I found myself dancing salsa, smoothly following my skilled leader. I learned from a man, Omar, that Cuban salsa differed from Puerto Rican salsa in having less forceful lyrics, "probably because we are not free to express ourselves," he speculated. But I found there was no dearth of self-expression this evening and everyone seemed to be a performing artist.

People sat on a stone ledge or the cobblestones. Guitars were strummed, rum was passed and poured down gullets. Israel sang *Perfidia* and *Hotel California*. Francisco, a jazz musician, grabbed the guitar and belted out a bluesy ballad. Osvaldo's laughter textured the night.

Suddenly it was after 1 AM, Francisco wanted a kiss and promise from me for mañana, Grace and Israel were speaking "Spanglish." He told her it is the most romantic thing in the world for a man to stroll the plaza with a lady on his arm. And Donna—my rum-enlivened baby sister who is five-feet-ten-inches tall—was sitting on the roof of the rented car, with Osvaldo urging her down.

"Donna, what are you doing up there?" I asked.

"I don't know," she said.

Thanks to Cuba's Committee for the Defense of the Revolution, I didn't have to be the heavy this time. The omnipresent policeman emerged out of the shadows and dressed down the men for disturbing the peace.

Leaving a trail of broken promises, we decided to head back to Havana the next day. By now, even Grace was game for picking up strangers. José, another self-proclaimed musician—as are most men in Trinidad—jumped into our backseat. We inquired about where to find the authentic Cuban coffee we'd experienced chez Delmis. "I know a place and it won't cost you anything." he said. A bit wary, we followed José to his Grandmother's house. Receiving us like friends she'd known for years, the silver-haired woman sat us in her living room where we could study her pagan-Catholic altar as she brewed coffee. Dollhouse cups of delicious black syrup were set before us. I stepped into the street to purchase some empanadas from a vendor to enjoy with the mind-altering beverage.

"Oh, I want to swallow the cup," whispered Donna as it disappeared in the palm of her hand.

On our way out of Trinidad, we passed horses, dogs, bikes, and children in mustard-colored uniforms. We saw vultures (Imperialists?) poised on a fence awaiting an opportunistic kill. Nearby white egrets rode horseback in a symbiotic (Socialists?) rapport. We were moved by two dogs lying atop an ill dog, obviously protecting or comforting it. Truly, the dog scene had this *only in Cuba* feel to it.

Back in Havana, with Delmis and Octavio and their boarders, we crowded around the dining room table. Everyone but me seemed to enjoy the pharmacological effects of nicotine or 150 proof.

"Que paso?" slurred Jorge a boarder from South America who spoke some English.

"I'm having mood swings," I answered. The next day, my sisters and I were heading home to our respective West and East coasts. "I'm counting the ways I can live without *hermanas*. And the ways I can't."

I wondered if we had accomplished enough in our ten days here in this forbidden-fruit country. Had we wasted too much time?

Jorge looked at me through rummy eyes and said, "I don't think she's a saint." I didn't think I was a saint either. I had merely given up drinking wine, my spirit of choice, for a year or I'd have joined in the revelry. However, sainthood aside, on some psychological level I wondered if my sisters and I were the trinity incarnate of Freud's map of the mind—Superego (me), Ego (Grace), and Id (Donna). Jorge was about to tease me again for refusing alcohol and tobacco, when a small incident brought a pregnant pause to the room—and blew my Freudian metaphor out of the water.

My sister Donna, who is as generous with others as she likes the world to be with her, removed her bracelet with the scorpions, roaches, and spiders suspended in Lucite. She handed it to Delmis as a good-bye gift. A change came over Delmis, whose Spanish was suddenly clear as white rum (she reclaimed her consonants). She began making quick excursions to her kitchen altar, where icons of Catholicism and Santeria, the spirituality of West Africa's Yoruba peoples (who were brought to Cuba as slaves), were scattered.

On each return to the dining room, Delmis brought something from her altar. First, she placed a necklace of bone-colored beads around Donna's neck and said this is from Oshun, goddess of love and money. Oshun loves to party, Delmis said, and is seductive. "She controls sensuality."

Delmis expounded on the power of orishas, or deities, as she placed a hand-woven bracelet on Grace's wrist. "Yemaya," she said, "is the queen of the sea. She rules over maternity—all life comes from water. Yemaya holds deep, unknowable secrets."

Finally, Delmis anointed me Orula. She leavened my separation anxiety with a smile and a strand of aquamarine beads around my neck. "Orula, orisha of medicine and healing does not fear death. He does not have a physical body."

"Hey, who needs *Makeover* without a body?" I said to Donna and Grace.

"Shhh. . . ," they both hushed me in a poignant display of role reversal. Delmis glowed. We glowed. We were being initiated by this unassuming woman who had

139

endured who knew what oppression. Yet, my sisters and I sparked the memory of her powers that no tyrant can oppress or diminish. Oshun, Yemaya, Orula. Our tongues twitched over wavy new syllables, as we each sensed a latent self, blossoming forth to the sounds. Suddenly the curls of tobacco smoke and fumes of hard spirits were sacred accessories—like wine and flatbread or burning candles and incense—to a sort of transubstantiation. In a way, I thought, doesn't all meaningful travel have this moment where you are you and no longer you? Maybe it's that you are more you than before. This was what we had come for.

My sisters and I humbly, silently contemplated our new identities and the magic of the impromptu ceremony. We had names aplenty for each other, to be sure. But on the altar—almost literally—of a richly layered culture, we were introduced to new, unknown selves. Now that is truly *la revolucion.*

10

Saving Grace, 2002

Snowmelt is a Western word. It's not one used by people in New Jersey. And it's not to be confused with the grungy, urban remnant that is more grime and car exhaust than snow. Ultraclean snowmelt is the glorious elixir that runs clear and cold from high granite keeps in the West. A hydrologist's brand of runoff, snowmelt is quintessential Western fare.

I wanted to introduce the flavor of snowmelt to my sister Grace, who's a bona fide east coaster. Each spring she calls. "Where's our trip this summer?" She trusts me to plan an adventure that will stretch her limits. So far I haven't failed her. The previous year I'd talked her through her fear of heights as we hiked up Yosemite Falls even while she nervously sang *I'll Take Manhattan.*

She wasn't ready to taste the champagne of melt that flows in the High Sierra. But I wanted her to know firsthand this regional specialty that drops from the heavens onto mountains below, only to transform in spring to muscular rivers, streams, and deep lakes. Snowmelt is something my sister will never experience in New Jersey.

I decided to take her to the far northern reaches of my adopted state, to the Trinity Alps, the fountainhead of copious snowmelt. Topping out at 9,000-foot Mount Thompson, the Alps are not as high as the Sierra. But

141

they've been just as worked over by the mighty glaciers that quarried basins and divides. The Alps are one of the most riven landscapes in California, drained by the Trinity, Scott, and Salmon rivers. In spring, the rivers and their mighty tributaries swell and seethe with the melting snows. Trinity County is rugged, remote, and beautified by vast tracts of old-growth forest. It has only five people per square mile, a human sparseness I deemed necessary for someone who lives near the mouth of the Lincoln Tunnel in Union City, part of a metropolis with the nation's densest head count.

Our first dunk came just an hour after we'd left the foggy redwood coast at Arcata. We traveled east on sunstruck 299, a highway so blessed with natural beauty it's been designated a national scenic byway. For 50 curving miles we lurched, trying to drive and devour the drama of forested mountains. The Trinity River, aptly labeled "wild and scenic," tumbled silver and frothy in its slot out our window. At last we pulled over at Cedar Flat and found a patch of sandy beach. The August sun was scorching, so it took us all of 30 seconds to let the Trinity's icy waters close over our heads. Reborn in the middle of a lazy green pool, I raised my arms to the sky and a steep oak-dotted riverbank and said, "Beats the Jersey shore, doesn't it?"

"It's different," Grace said. It's not that she wasn't impressed. Just that she's a diehard defender of her own backyard.

"Wait 'til tomorrow," I promised, swallowing a Cheshire cat grin.

Weaverville's treelined main street features old spiral staircases; the Joss House, a Taoist temple rebuilt from ashes in 1873; and a drugstore which opened its doors in 1854. We stopped where 299 bisects another national scenic byway, Highway 3, in Weaverville, the county seat. We checked into the old Weaverville Hotel, which has a lot of yesteryear charm—perhaps too much, in its weak shower nozzle and soft beds. Grace's bed sheets had sand in them. I suggested she feel honored—it might have dated back to the town's Gold Rush era, left by some forlorn prospector.

At the crack of dawn, we plumped up our backpacks with snacks and water bottles and headed to our trailhead at Bridge Camp.

The Stuart Fork of the Trinity courses through the stunning emerald landscape of Morris Meadow on its downstream journey. The round-trip hike to Morris is some 16 miles. I told Grace, "It's 10 miles." This wasn't an abuse of power, decreed to me by birth order (I'm still and forever one year and four days older). Just part of our annual ritual. Remember Yosemite?—she came back. We headed past huckleberries and ferns, shaded by black oaks, Douglas fir, and Jeffrey pines.

"The Stuart's waters start as snowpack in the 'White Trinities,' the untracked heart of the Alps," I primed her from Wayne Moss's *The Trinity Alps Companion*. I had

143

many hours to distract my sister from counting miles as we strolled the long canyon.

We had swimming opportunities to distract us, too, but decided to save one for the return trip. At Deer Creek, the spray from a cascade teased us. I took a photo of Grace, standing on the bridge over the pool of snowmelt. She was still smiling. We reminisced about the good times before I took the fork up ahead in the road.

We were once practically Siamese twins. In early childhood, she became the gregarious one and I was quiet and timid, qualities that worried my parents so much they sent me to acrobatic school when I was five.

One day when Grace and I were eleven and twelve, our childhood as we knew it ended. Mom had to take a job at a factory around the corner, Grace Holmes, to help pay the bills. From then on, Grace and I were expected to rush home from St. Mary's grammar school and cook supper. (To this day my best cooking is any meal that can feed twelve people.) At first, I admit it was thrilling. But then it became a chore that curtailed play. We were told to look after the little ones, but I recall that I neglected them, being too preoccupied with when I might get to see my friends. I recall my little sister Lisa being hungry. All I could find were pickles and peanut butter, which I gave her. Lisa still has a fond memory of the combination.

Grace and I had actually started working when we were eight and nine. We split one of our brother's newspaper routes, delivering the *Elizabeth Daily Journal* on foot after school. Sometimes we received seventy-five cents allowance from the tips, a huge sum for us. But then, someone reported seeing girls deliver papers and we were forced to stop. It was one case of sexism that I didn't mind.

Summers, confined to our block, we found ways to entertain ourselves besides the stick and kick ball all the kids played. Grace and I got together with friends, Kathy and Liz Bodnar, Helen Burt, Joanne Basile, and put on a show in our backyard. Kathy and I worked out a jazz number to *Sugar Shack*. Lizzie sang *The Lady in Red*. Helen Burt who was plump and had strong lungs sang a beautiful *Somewhere Over the Rainbow*. Little sister Tina came in handy—we worked her into our act and had her do aerials with two of us as ballerinas. We hung a bedspread over Mom's clothesline for the stage, used Jim's laboratory as our dressing room, and set up picnic benches for all of our paying guests. We did two shows on the big day, one at night for our parents who worked.

We also put on a carnival each summer with games, prizes, and even a funhouse in the Bodnars' dark garage. We pushed kids around blindfolded in an old desk chair, made them feel "worms," (cold spaghetti), tickled them with feathery gossmer, played *Monster Mash* and scared them to their delight. We made enough money at these enterprises to go to Olympic or Palisades amusement parks, adventures second only to going down the shore.

The best times of our lives together were our teens. Grace and I started hanging out with Kathy and Chris who introduced us to Bauer's and the Super Diner, hangouts in downtown Rahway where we met tough-talking boys in leather jackets, cigarettes hanging off their lips, with something thick and anxious in the air that my Catholic schooling kept me from recognizing: SEX.

But it was with Kathy and Chris we had the best times. We called ourselves The Groupe. With a quick and dirty alibi, Grace and I escaped Sunday's boring afternoons with *la familia* to meet Chris and Kathy at the Cross Keys, a bar that let in underage kids but never served us. On the Keys' dance floor we all created a line dance to *Mustang Sally*.

All through high school, the four of us told our parents we were going to the library at night. To keep from having to confess the lie to the priest, we always set foot in the library, then went and hung out for hours with the public school kids. Some of the boys called us the Blessed Trinity (although we were four, not three) because we didn't put out. I was proud of our reputation.

Then my first year of college I had a huge awakening. I realized that I was the only one not going all the way. Grace, eighteen and pregnant with Tanya, married Art although I begged her not to—we have so much to live for yet, I might have said. My view of marriage was not a positive one. I might still be hanging out at the Super Diner if Grace hadn't married. Meanwhile, wanting nothing to do with marriage yet, I waited until I was twenty-and-a-half. I took a deep psychological breath, then went all the way with Eddie B., whose stuffy family apartment in Harrison was near a Schickhaus hot dog factory—at least that has always been the overriding memory, possibly false, of that otherwise unmemorable rite of passage.

In time I came to like Grace's husband, Art, very much. Art went from being a guy who re-upped for three tours of Nam in the Green Beret to a health food nut who to this day eschews, white flour, refined sugar, caffeine, and alcohol. His transformation has always inspired admiration. Tanya, my "goddesschild," and then Scott, her brother, made me a happy aunt. Grace and Art remained married some twenty years and then, as often happens with early marriages, they grew apart. Now I have Grace back to myself whenever I can plan a trip that seduces her. Like this one here in Trinity.

We have that uncanny communication of twins and close siblings. We can dialog without ever speaking. But when she was still smiling, as we reached Morris Meadow with its waist-high grasses, I wondered if we had been apart for too long. She suspected nothing of my ruse.

Beyond a copse of willows, alders, and incense cedars, a horse whinnied at a packers camp, and I knew we both wished we could laze for hours, staring at the tilting slabs of Sawtooth Mountain. But we had to return to a certain gravel bar where the Stuart took a break from its fierce crashing in rock channels to run slack. Retracing our steps, we passed anglers, fishing for rainbows. Then, long past the flashpoint of calf burn and hot feet, we saw our bank, lined with cottonwoods and big-leaf maples.

"The harder the hike, the greater the reward," I sighed as we sank into the soothing waters. Shadowy fish sidled by. The river and vegetation smelled tart and fresh, but Grace's smile looked wilted. We draped ourselves over smooth granite and she said, "This is more than 10 miles."

"What was your first clue?" I asked, triumphant.

"We've passed a dozen hikers. We're the only ones doing this trip in one day."

True, most backpackers camped at Morris and took day hikes to Emerald, Sapphire, and Mirror lakes.

"I knew you could do it," I said. "You ran a marathon."

"Ten years ago."

"I'll get you back in one piece."

Or would I?

As I plowed ahead alone at my own swifter pace, I suddenly recalled that short story we had to read in ninth grade at Mother Seton, *The Scarlet Ibis*. I have been ever since occasionally and darkly haunted by the story that begins with the epigram, *". . . pride is a wonderful, terrible thing, a seed that bears two vines, life and death."* In the story by James Hurst, the narrator, an adolescent, has a younger brother with some sort of physical defect from birth. That does not stop the narrator from rabid bouts of what I knew to be sibling rivalry. I identified with his constant need for one-upmanship, for childish forms of cruelty, a type of passive-aggressive punishment for a sibling who had the nerve, the unforgivable chutzpah to show up while we were still tender young things ourselves. In 1965 when I read the story I had never heard of the term sibling rivalry, nor was there any psychology in the air, in our neighborhood at least, for toddlers who suddenly find themselves replaced. The narrator, Brother, pushes his sibling, Doodle, the way I pushed Grace. But eventually Brother causes Doodle to pay the ultimate price, pushing him too hard, way beyond Doodle's capacity. It is such a sad, beautiful story and I can never think of it without feeling tears form and identifying with the terrible remorse of Brother, not to mention the unfortunate abandonment of Doodle.

As I hiked, I hoped to not see a dead bird along the way, the way the scarlet ibis appears in the story, having lost its way and dying bleeding far from home, a dark foreshadowing of what was to come to the fragile Doodle. As I waited what seemed an interminably long time for my still living (I trusted) younger sibling, I was haunted by the heart-wrenching last words spoken by Doodle, *"Brother, Brother, don't leave me! Don't leave me!"*

Some nine hours after we'd started, I breathed a sigh of relief and *The Scarlet Ibis* returned to its airtight storage unit in my underground memory bank, completely forgotten until the next revisit.

Here came Grace, walking like a wooden soldier whose knees wouldn't bend.

"You did it," I cheered feebly.

"Yeah, but I may not walk for a week."

But I knew, in her mind she was already bragging to the flatlanders back East: "You won't believe the river canyon my sister and I hiked." At least that's what I wanted to believe and it made me feel better.

Once again Grace had proved her mettle. Now came the pampering. The Carrville Inn, with its gracious Victorian and frontier spirit, would spoil the most jaded of my five sisters. We pulled up on the old California-Oregon Stage Road, boots caked with earth. We couldn't have looked worse than Herbert Hoover did when he lodged here—after doing some local mining engineer work.

The Carrville Inn is the 1850s legacy of James E. Carr, owner of mining claims in Trinity County. Today, it is a sumptuous bed-and-breakfast.

The inn, rebuilt in 1917 after fire destroyed the 1854 structure, gleamed against evergreens, old oaks, apple and cherry trees. A weathered barn burbled with farm animals. A trail led to the Carr family graveyard with its moss-eaten headstones, including those of four children who died of diphtheria in the 1800s.

Owners Sheri and Dave Overly had left Stockton behind for the inn's country elegance. In the morning, over Sheri's baked French toast, we met the other guests. A couple, who had flown their plane from San Jose to Trinity Center, dissed Grace with a standard barb about Jersey. But she took to Dave Drewry, who owned the llamas in the corral. He rhapsodized about a pack trip with his outfit, Como Say Llamas, to Mumford Meadow, where he'd spotted a golden eagle. When Grace heard that the llamas carry all of the cargo, she made sure I got Dave's brochure for any future hike I had in mind.

That night, we lay spent in our twin beds in the Carrville's Hoover Room, the stillness broken only by insects and prowling animals. We thought of blood-curdling shrieks that pierced the night as we camped at the start of our trip. "Maybe it was Bigfoot," I whispered.

"He could've been more considerate," Grace yawned.

"Dozens of Bigfoot sightings have been reported in this area," I said. "I hear he wails like a mountain lion." Feeble attempts to tell scary stories lulled us to sleep. I half-awoke to a persistent sound. My sister was a deep sleeper, so I wondered why she was flapping. When she started to squeal I got annoyed, opened my eyes, and saw a half dozen black shadows circling overhead. Bats. They'd flown in through a window. I bolted for the door and Grace stirred.

"Why are you standing in the doorway with a pillowcase over your head?" she asked groggily.

"Umm," I said.

She gasped, "BATS!!!" Her head vanished under the covers. With some coaxing, Grace ran out of the room. We grabbed our sleeping bags from the car and threw them on the floor in the Rose Room. Next morning, I sat on the sunny porch, sipped coffee, and watched finches flit around Shasta daisies. Grace appeared and said, "They're back."

"Bats sleep all day," I said.

151

"They are asleep—all around the room." By and by, Sheri joined us, shooing the creatures out the window with a towel and I saw that they'd had the guano scared out of them. Sheri and I wanted my sister from the Wrong Coast to appreciate these shy, beneficial insect-eaters. "Grace," Sheri said, "you have to see this." Grace inched her way over to the bathroom to see a bat hanging from the rafter. "Isn't that cute!" But the bat let go and Grace ran like a you-know-what out of hell.

The bats had been seeking the attic and missed their mark. But, thanks to our visit they flew the coop and Sheri installed screens in all the windows.

Where the snowmelt runs, so do the fish, thus I'd arranged a half-day of guided fly-fishing. Water diversion by the Trinity Dam has all but destroyed the once great salmon and steelhead fishing of the area, but Fish and Game plants Eastern brook trout and rainbow, golden, and brown trout. But my quest was single-minded—to stand enraptured in nature's dark, mystical, liquid currency.

"Where shall we have the seminar?" asked the guide, whom I'll call Jed Pescatore. I looked around at snowy peaks and virgin stands. The evening before, Grace and I had seen just how far this untouched wilderness stretched as we cruised Highway 3. Pines gave way to chaparral basted with the amber sunlight of the Golden State. We climbed over Scott Mountain, went through Callahan and Etna, gateway to the Marble Mountain Wilderness, and still hadn't run out of wilds, some of it accessible only on trails worn by prospectors, trappers, and ranchers.

"Just take us to a pretty spot on the Trinity," I urged.

Jed replied, "That's indicative of ignorance of the sport."

He had a point. I'd cast a fly line maybe a dozen times. Three hours and 23 pages of photocopy later, my glaze-eyed sister and I had learned, among other things, the life cycles of nymphs, caddis flies, and mayflies—zilch about fly-tying. Jed gave us 15 minutes of land practice, roll- and back-casting, then led us to a treeless spot on the Trinity. He stood behind us and cast our arms for us. We each caught tiny trout, which Jed released for us. Exhausted and disappointed, we paid and begged him to leave.

Jed in no way typified other locals we met in Trinity, like our waitress at the Forest Cafe in Coffee Creek, who told us to visit Alpen Cellars, Trinity's only winery. But we were endlessly way laid by the next icy plunge. A shaded curve on the North Fork, tucked off 299, had perhaps no fish to catch, but all the allure that earns the Alps their name. It was just past Helena, a ghost town with an overgrown post office, brewery, farmhouse, and cottages. We soaked until we turned blue, then baked on sauna-warm boulders. Little eddies sang over polished pebbles, a water ouzel dunked nervously, and everything unfolded according to plan. What's one guide from hell?

Grace cried when we checked out of Carrville Inn. "Look, you gotta toughen up," I said, "if you want to come back to Trinity." And with that I hiked her up to Boulder Lakes, during which Mount Shasta rammed the horizon with its sun-brightened snowcap.

Then we discovered a parallel universe along the snow-fed Coffee Creek, where thousands of miners once lived and dredged for gold. Happily, they didn't mine the breathtaking vistas of peaks, cascades, and meadows with browsing deer. After checking into Coffee Creek Resort, we joined families and the dude ranch owners, Ruth and Mark Hartman, for dinner. Ruth tended her 127-acre resort with the cumulative wisdom of a fourth-generation Californian. It was easy to sense the Old West in her corral where an Appaloosa and thoroughbreds had been raised from colts.

The Hartmans had just returned from New Orleans, so we feasted on crawfish, blackened catfish, jambalaya, and bread pudding. Ruth had also brought back ghost tales from the bayou, which piqued the interest of my sister, who is sporadically psychic. (For example, her father-in-law appeared on her TV at the time he was dying.)

Ruth spoke of the resort ghost, Harold, who like many lone ghosts, is more mischievous than frightening. He must have seen us coming: Grace and I headed to the faux-granite Jacuzzi. As we were pummeled by jets, the electricity went dead and we bobbed in silence and black primal soup. I tried to feel my way to the ledge, but a force weighed me down. It was my sister. She was spooked. The lights came on with no explanation. "If it's not bats, it's Harold saying hello," said Grace.

We couldn't join Ruth's party for a morning gallop in God's country and breakfast on the trail because we had a long drive to San Francisco. We headed south on Highway 3, stopping at the dam's handsome viewing deck.

"It looks like an ocean." said Grace, surveying the artificial lake's 145 miles of auburn dirt shoreline.

"It's a manmade guzzler of snowmelt," I said. "It reroutes 90 percent of the Alps' watershed to the Sacramento Valley."

"So they can put eight great tomatoes in that little bitty can," said Grace who was weaned on Contadina's TV commercials. A dot on the wide blue expanse turned into a water skier on this watery grave for meadows, ranches, and native Wintu history. Loath to depart, we sat on the redwood planks and paged through local real estate listings. We found a dwelling and acreage selling for less than two months' city rent.

We haven't followed up. Yet. But my sister, who is, after all, psychic, called the other day. Over the roar of Lincoln Tunnel traffic I heard her say, "I see a deep pool of snowmelt in our near future."

11

In the Land of Milk and Honey

The Marin Headlands are truly urban wilds. They are connected intimately to the City of San Francisco by that ripe-persimmon *em* dash, the Golden Gate Bridge. The amphibious hills are wild and protected national land. I've cycled across the bridge and done the rigorous headlands loop thousands of times, always mornings, before the wind kicks up.

Cycling this roller coaster ocean-side route I am fully in my mind and body. Each of those thousands of rides has been a hero's journey for me. My epiphanies, big and small, and subtle transformations occur here amid muscle power and concentration. Amid beauty and views of the bridge and ocean and city I love. Atop Hawk Hill I sit on a pew-bench in my church of peace and harmony, watching the hills taper out to sea like a crawling crocodile poised to strike. Careless visitors have slipped to their death on occasion and more than once I have come upon death by bicycle in those hills.

My route begins near the San Francisco Marina. Atop a hill at Fort Mason. It's as if I'm looking through a wide-angle lens that takes in the full span of the bridge, the bay with its fleets of shining sailboats, the headlands, which I see under the bridge. From up on the Marina Green, I see clear through an underarm, an arch of the bridge to Point Bonita, the tip of the headlands (the croc's head) where there is an old lighthouse and nesting pelicans, cormorants, and pigeon guillemots that roost on guano-stained rock with a cave and ocean roiling all around it. On clear winter days, I can almost see on the bridge towers the rivets that remind me of Braille.

In that first wide-angle frame, I see war and peace, life and death, the beginning of time, the origin of species and evolution on land, air, and sea. I know that all of that is there from having climbed those chunky hills so many times and looked and focused a little deeper each time, occasionally startled by the likes of a resident quail family, a cougar, rabbit, or a red-shouldered hawk.

Cycling the Marin Headlands is pulse raising, morale boosting, and soul centering, psychotherapeutic. They are my mind-altering drugs, my mood elevating elixir. The burnt sugar of the bridge, the thick cream of fog, and its basso profundo horn dwell in me permanently by now. Everyone needs a route that intuits the homeland of her whole life; no matter how mobile you are you find this. It must be accessible daily.

The headlands are my Land of Milk and Honey, which was once one of California's nicknames.

I have developed a lexicon of fog, a Fog-logue. *Zencurls* are wayseeking fog, *tendrilli* are spirals of fog, *luxoria* is light-saturated fog. We have *snow,* flaky fog that resembles a blizzard in progress. I have dozens of other names, just as the Eskimos have hundreds of names for real snow. Fog and its ever-shifting intercourse with light is richly, lyrically nuanced. Although I have yet to see its *cat feet*, Mr. Sandburg. Well, maybe I have.

One Sunday morning, I am besieged by uncertainty, that dull lonely ache of feeling I should be somewhere else—in my yoga temple, swimming in the bay, dancing, writing, communing with any of my many urban tribes. A few minutes into my bike ride, a flock of wild parrots squawk overhead and catch the sun on their pistachio green and yellow plumage flitting between the palms in Fort Mason. Perhaps it is those made famous in the film about the escaped tribe of parrots who live nearby on Telegraph Hill. Their welcome intrusion cancels all uncertainty. I am right where I belong. This is why when I feel lonely I go to the headlands, preferably alone.

This morning, I ride into winter's rose-petal sunrise and breeze through the cables and strings, admiring the long cigar shadows cast by rivets on the towers, pedaling like an angelic messenger on a giant harp. The steep rocky hills are alive with precocious wildflowers—a fetching bouquet of golden poppies, scarlet Indian paintbrush, purple lupine, pink checker bloom (spring comes in winter more and more). A field trip of geology students investigates the Franciscan Complex, chocolate-y layers in the headland roadcuts. Each of those three-inch slabs compresses more lifetimes than there are people in California. I pass the Van Gogh (my name) rock with its bold rippling lines in the sun. The "picture window" provides a view back to the city, there before I come

158

upon the bunkers that were built during World War II. A sign reads Mortars to Missiles—there were mortars, disappearing guns, and Nike Missiles here. The Nikes were operational until 1974. The sign says the headlands have been instrumental in war since the Spanish-American through the Cold War.

I have taken three of my four brothers to nurse from the breast of those hills with their placid relics of war.

Salvatore, the most bellicose-inclined of the four, works on cutting-edge (no pun intended) laser technology at Kirtland Air Force Base in Albuquerque. He visits me one day while on business in the area. The Granola Bowl—take away the fruits and the nuts and all you have left are the flakes—suits Sal's opinion of my city. Salvatore is the only person I know who finds aloha, the spirit of Hawaii, suspect, a turnoff. Give Sal New York surliness any day,

The only thing to do, the only way to keep our wildly heated political arguments at bay, which I no longer care to indulge in, is to take him outdoors. Make him move.

"Want to see the Land of Milk and Honey, Sal?"

"Sure, let's go."

One thing I can say about my whole tribe, all are poised for motion. Not one of us is a couch potato. In my dime-store analysis of that attribute, I think movement, at times excessive in a few of is, is our drug of choice for the anxiety we felt as kids with Dad's mood swings, which were his own anxiety about providing for the lot of us. Or just the result of the ordinary chaos that was inevitable with that many bodies squeezed together. (We are Dad's heirs apparent to a rich mother lode of anxiety.) We once prayed together, ate together, danced together, laughed and cried together.

Salvatore behaves best in my view when we share the outdoors experience. He once hiked me up Sandia Peak in Albuquerque and I recall his sweeping gesture over the natural beauty we both loved and were moved by. He attributed it to his patriarchal God. I did not argue, although I long ago internalized the equally devout belief about that God: "Who has seen God cannot describe him/her/it, who can describe him/her/it, has not seen him/her/it."

Given the opportunity, Sal would taunt me for my liberal values. In the pecking order I'm right after Sal. The oft-told family story is that Mom believed she was done having kids after Salvatore, number four, was born. She wanted only four. But three years later I came, fulfilling the prediction of "a devout Catholic, Murphy's sister," as my parents tell it. Then came the five others every other year. Curiously, my parents and all nine of my siblings were born on even years. I, the only left-handed child, was born on an odd year. Another curious statistic: Dad and five of the ten kids are born between January 27 and February 20: hence one big birthday party in winter sufficed.

The ten kids in our family seem to have organically divided into five units of two—Grace and I were one, Jim and Terry, and Chuck and Sal, for example. I was always interested in what Sal and Chuck were up to. They built wooden hot rods that I got a ride in once. They built a wooden fort in our backyard, with no roof though. They told jokes that were on you and teased and were masters of "got you last" and running off after tapping you. They did swats to any one of the boys who had just got a haircut—swiping the back of the head. They taught me that silly *You remind me of a man. What man? Man of the power. What power? Power of who-do. Who do what? You do. I do what? You remind me of a man. What man?* Which I now think was my first peek into philosophy of the absurd, or pre-existentialism.

When Salvatore wasn't *pecking* on me, he helped me with my science. One unforgettable year, my sixth grade, his ninth, he helped me with my science project for Mrs. Meyers class. I can still taste the bitter desire to beat out the boy allegedly the smartest in our class, Larry C., who was also vying to get his project into the science fair. Sal and I spent nearly a month of late evenings assembling my idea—all the ways we use electricity. I fashioned a primitive motor, an armature with a dry cell, nails, wooden board and wires, to show motion. I wired the cell to a light bulb. I made a littler radiator, like the ones in our home, with aluminum foil for heat. I even sprayed the cardboard of it silver with spray paint once used for my dance recital shoes. Finally, still not thinking it all good enough, I asked Sal to help me take apart our Master Mind computer game and reassemble it as a computer in which you insert question tabs like how much is 2 + 2, and the correct answer lights up. Yes, I was overdoing it, but Sal and I were having long, calm, serene school nights creating this monster—or monstrosity, as Mrs. Meyers would call it. The night before the deadline to submit projects, I still wanted to improve it. I bought a huge piece of oak tag from Ducoff's downtown on Cherry Street and using old paints from a paint by number set, my mother and I painted what was supposed to be water falls giving us hydro-electricity. That fateful morning, I couldn't walk the mile to school with my Frankenstein, so I got a ride somehow with the unwieldy project. I knew I was going to be the ONE to have her project submitted in the fair. I just knew it. So I placed the whole thing in the front of the room next to Mrs. Meyers' desk. When Mrs. Meyers finally arrived she asked me to get "this mess out of my way." It's for the Science Fair, I told her. She informed me snappily that Larry C.'s project was already entered. His project was less than a foot wide—a weather vane. The simplicity of it was beautiful and elegant, I now know. I was totally embarrassed by my messy contraptions and took it all home where it gathered dust and decay, as did my interest in science until much later in life when I regretted deeply not pushing through all the lack of encouragement girls got in my days.

Sal and I will always have science. Years later when I self-educated on quantum physics he gave me a helpful volume, *Understanding Physics*, by Isaac Asimov. He patiently explained control theory to me. But we will likely never have politics or religion. So be it.

Today Salvatore refrains from promoting his archconservative politics. Even though he is a scientist, I'm afraid he would take the side of the Creationists so we won't marvel over the leather-jacket evolution that hangs out all over my headlands. Sal enjoys the challenging ride. We take it slow over the Golden Gate. Sal wants to gaze out at the ocean-going vessels. We ponder the not infrequent bridge-jumping that is never publicized, although I have seen the smoke bombs thrown into the current after someone jumps and seen the fire trucks futile but requisite arrival at Fort Point.

We ride in silence a lot. I recall another defining moment in our family, when the muscle of all four brothers was required. Dad was on his own suicide spiral after his early retirement at age 51, with his war-injured back pain too far gone. He blossomed into full-fledged alcoholism over the next eight years, the most miserable in the history of my family. A year into his self-destructive drinking, I left the east coast for San Francisco, in part to get as far away as possible from the crazy times. When my three youngest sisters, Lisa, Tina, and Donna, who were too young to leave home yet, tell of Dad's behavior in those days, my hair stands straight up for hours. Some day they will write that book. Eight years into his retirement, the eve of my brother Tom's wedding, Dad became spectacularly inebriated. We were all lodging at a Holiday Inn in Massachusetts where the bride's family lived. At first it was lugubriously funny. Dad slurring, told me he wanted to learn about Buddhism. I laughed. Then shortly later there was incredible chaos. Jim, Chuck, Sal, and Tom, along with Mom's brother, Uncle Pat, were wrestling my incoherent father to the floor, wresting the handgun away from him, which they dismantled and threw into a river. Hearts were pumping, Mom was raging. All for the last time. Dad had hit his rock bottom and was deeply mortified beyond words the next day, as well as suffering badly from the DTs. My mother gave him a sip of alcohol in the room where we had locked him—and later learned that she may have saved his life. Jim, now the child who is father to the man, paid for Dad to get into the best rehab, Carrier Clinic in New Jersey. For the next twenty-five years, the remainder of his life on earth, Dad didn't touch alcohol. At times he was a paragon of kindness, wisdom, and generosity. Other times, he was still a dry drunk, headstrong, nasty, grandiose, pontificating, irrational. We sentient beings are all complicated, aren't we? Such are the scenes my brothers, sisters, and I have lived through.

Sal is grateful for the bike ride and lets me know. He makes his trademark sweeping arm gesture and gives his God the credit for it. I'm tempted to say *But it's Mount Olympus* and has numerous gods, that his one-God truism is stultifying. I don't argue. God, Cosmic Consciousness, the One—as long as we are not killing in Its name, fine. He might have made his usual taunt about my politics, then added "but I love you anyway." Some say he is most like my father—not in being violent, but in being headstrong. Donna recalls how Sal would swallow a slice of Wonder Bread whole. The image fits. The rest of us balled up the doughy center first. They also say Sal is like my mother's father, Sam (ne Salvatore), who was gentle, observant, and could fix any machine or thing-a-ma-jig known to man. He could even invent things.

This evening after our bike ride Sal takes his family, Dan, and me out to eat at Kuleto's on Union Square for good food and wine. We can fight like archenemies over religion and politics but we are not above coming home happily to the way we were to break bread, communing in our imperfect ways. Prodigal sons and daughters we are.

Thanksgiving, not Christmas, was the sacrosanct holiday in our home. No matter what else we eat, to this day there has to be ravioli. One Thanksgiving Dan and I decide to host the West Coast family, who expect the usual homemade ravis preceding the turkey and other typical American foods. Let me cut to the chase: We buy the "homemade" ravis from a place that seems promising. They cook up like mush and are edible if you can scrape them off the roof of your mouth. Dan and I never live down the year of the mushy ravioli.

But there is the great bike ride to my headlands. Thanksgiving morning, Dan and I take two other brothers, Chuck and Tom, riding over the bridge to the glorious headlands. Chuck and especially Tom are strong riders. While Chuck and I bond and bicker in the

165

backcountry, Tom and I have done the Donner Lake Triathlon together every July, with his four children supporting us. Tom regularly rides up the steep East Bay Mount Diablo, which winks across the bay at viewers at the top of the headlands.

I emphasize my warnings about exercising caution on the roller coaster down side of the headlands from Hawk Hill. I've seen three men spill head over heels with their bikes. One of them was Dan, who spilled in slow motion over his handlebars and was miraculously only bruised. One was a friend, Allen, who suddenly vanished from my view. Only his bike on the roadside with spinning wheels remained. As I spun around searching for him, he popped up like a jack-in-the-box from the sagebrush on the slope, scratched and bleeding but not seriously injured. I watched another man come up conscious but bleeding from the head after he flipped on the pavement and I left him in the charge of a CHP who was having a hard time convincing him he needed medical attention. And yet another time the steep one-way downhill was closed with a policeman guarding the road. An experienced cyclist just in front of me had spilled on the curving turn and died from his injury. Nor was that the last—some time later, I watched a bold helmet-less young man take his last ride on this planet in that same spot. You might think the area has a Bermuda-Triangle-esque spell. But it doesn't. These deaths are "pilot" error.

Despite all this, Tom, an avid triathlete, tells me he was prepared for a worse incline than what I had described. Good. Human error aside, I have been there when the hills took good young men. I like to tease Tom about the first time I took him on a hike in the headlands. Suddenly he was running backwards up the hill like a fractured flicker. We had come upon a king snake. Tom looked quite funny. I could tease him a lot more at one time, when we were young and he was shorter than me and I could keep his retaliatory blows at a distance just by holding his head back in my palm. Now he towers over me at 6'4" so fortunately for me we only spar verbally. He has yet to come backpacking with Chuck and me. His wife Patty says, he likes to change his clothes often. Which is good fodder for an occasional tease.

Ironically, this Thanksgiving Day, Dan Chuck, Tom, and I witness another sort of death scene. We have safely completed the loop and are crossing the Golden Gate Bridge heading home. A man is lying on the sidewalk of the bridge where only cyclists, no pedestrians are allowed. He is surrounded by people. An ambulance is there. Though smack in the middle of the bridge, which has no shoulder, the man must have had time to considerately pull his pickup over. He has apparently had a heart attack. He can't be more than early forties. He is handsome and he has on his boots—maybe he is a carpenter or construction worker. The paramedics are administering CPR, but he is purple. The paramedics make cyclists get off their bikes and walk them past the fallen man. The news that evening confirms his death on the bridge. No pilot error, his.

A family visit back east follows some time later. It was not relaxing, as I had planned. When I arrived from the airport, Mom and Dad didn't hear me walk in their Annapolis home until I was right on top of them. The TV that's as big as my water closet back home was blasting. Never mind things that go bump in the night, the scary sounds coming all day long in my family's homes. But Mom and Dad's home takes the prize. I'm not sure how many of their clocks (which they cannot hear) sound on the hour, two or three, but it seems like a dozen because one of them plays a different song each hour. *Unchained Melody, Around the World in 80 days, Stardust* comes from a music box. Electric coffee pots creak, microwaves ping, all appliances unwelcome in my home. One morning I awaken to a shrill ear-piercing beep. My mother is sitting in the kitchen saying her rosary undisturbed by the drilling noise. "It's the battery in the carbon monoxide detector," she says. "I can't get it out." She continues quietly with her rosary as the phone rings loud enough to blow me back to San Francisco. I head to my sister Tina's home in Bethlehem, Pennsylvania, where the plinks, plunks, and fairy dust sounds of computers are less torture. I'm alone in her home listening to the sweet birdsong in her back yard when I hear a high-pitched baby voice singing *Sesame Street*. It is coming from their living room. Over and over. It is the dog quietly playing with his toy. He bites the middle of the red fuzzy thing and it sings nonstop. I walk over to the cage where the other dog, a ten-month-old border collie, is left while the whole family is out. The collie growls at me. Wilderness begins at home.

First thing I do back home in San Francisco is hit the headlands on my bike. Another day, another hero's journey. The aloneness of it is welcome. The hills are alive with the poetry of my life, my otherwise meaningless existence. The *Odyssey* begins with Odysseus praying to the muse of poetry. I have read that for the ancient Greeks poetry was what lent immortality to the people whose stories the poem captured. Poetry for them was a mysterious and godlike art that required supernatural help. My headlands are super and they are natural. They giveth life, they taketh away. They are the living poem where my many stories are writ. Please do fling my ashes here. Amen.

12

Old Italians Don't Die, 1993

My father and Uncles Val and Joe are gathered around the huge barbecue grill as one of them flips the burgers and hot dogs. Dad wears a T-shirt that flaunts the Italian and American flags and reads something catchy about being a proud Italian. Uncle Joe wears one with an etching of Christopher Columbus on it. "They want to say he was a bad guy now," Joe says about the sudden groundswell of bad press Columbus has gotten. The men all shake their heads and look more hurt than anything. They've all been initiated into the Knights of Columbus, an honor that had the added bonus of having been extended to them by Irishmen, the previous immigrant community in America's pecking order.

At one time, Dad would have gotten on his soapbox about the "denigration" of Italians and gone through a roster of their great contributions to this country, including how Thomas Jefferson wanted Italian, not English, to be our national language (a "fact" too good for me to check). Now the men stand around in baggy bermudas, T-shirts tucked out over bellies, and non-slip rubber-soled shoes or sandals. They speak in their father tongue that eludes me. They allude to theirs and others' medical problems in near *sottovoce*, because just yesterday that chatter was not manly.

The picnic tables are laden with typical American barbecue food—hot dogs, burgers, sauerkraut, white bread, potato salad. Only the sausage and meatballs hint at our heritage. The women sit calmly chatting. I can't tell how many are bored, biding time, and wish they were elsewhere but have shown up because the ritual of *la familia*, has such *centripetal* force. I conclude with a sighing mixture of sadness and surrender, *Old Italians don't die, they become American.*

It is the summer of 1993 and this is my first attendance at the annual Federico-Fascella picnic that brings some three or four generations of about thirty to forty of us relatives together. The picnic is held at the Gran Centurions, Clark, New Jersey, a private club founded in 1966 by Italians "To foster and perpetuate the rich heritage of Italian ancestry, culture and history." By mere coincidence, I once worked a catering shift here back when I was trying to save money to escape from New Jersey.

At first my father refused to attend the picnic because it was not called The *Cusumano*-Federico picnic. He made his patriarchal stink and then deigned to appear. Federico is his mother's maiden name. Fascella is his grandmother's maiden name. One way or another all of us are connected to his father, my grandfather, Vincenzo Cusumano (who became James in this country, don't ask me *why not Vincent*). Grandpa sailed from Hamburg in April, 1903, on the *Palatia*. He had his mother with him but she did not like *l'America* so she returned to *la bella Sicilia*. Most of the

171

native-born Italians in my family came through Ellis Island, many arriving on ships third class. They made their way to Peterstown, still the Italian enclave in Elizabeth Port, New Jersey. My father grew up there, his first language Sicilian, in a household with aunts, uncles, cousins, some sixteen people under one roof. My mother lived around the corner but they did not meet until she was sixteen. Dad and my mother's mother, Grandma Catalano had the textbook in-law relationship, with strong animus between them for years. Grandma Cats, or Meatball Grandma (she was short and round), was one tough biscotti who would have picked a man less romantic and more practical than Dad to marry Carmela. They married when she was nineteen, in July 1941, and in December, when Pearl Harbor was bombed, he was shipped off to New Guinea in the Army Air Corps, not to return for nearly two years.

I have not been at many family reunions since I left New Jersey—ran from it—for California in 1973 in a Chevy van with less than a hundred dollars in my pocket. So I haven't been around to watch my Italian clan slowly become *'merican*. While I was being re-molded in the crucible of San Francisco's Haight-Ashbury hippiedom, practicing vegetarianism, communal living, supporting social-minded food co-ops, boycotting table grapes and iceberg lettuce, and protesting war, nukes, and conventional materialism, my Italian family was climbing the social ladder, moving to the burbs, packing their sub-zero freezers with red meat, hot dogs, and white bread.

172

It's as if I expected them to stay frozen in a frame I have of them from years ago.

Two conversations dominate my interactions with my aunts. "Honey, when am I going to come to your wedding?" I usually have a smart answer for that one. The truth is that I have nothing against marriage and children but they are way down my list. I am intimate with life on my own terms and no regrets there. The second topic concerns my oldest brother, Jim, a whispered slur on his wife. No one is ever good enough for their nephew, the clan's firstborn, who bears their father's name. While my siblings and I may gossip about each other, we don't countenance such bad mouthing with "outsiders." So, I just shrug my shoulders and stab a sausage link with a fork. "They are perfect yin and yang," I say of Jim and his wife, referring to his dark features and her fair ones. A cousin exclaims to me, "You're eating meat!?"

I wince under her disappointment. She has expected me to remain the hippie vegetarian I once was, the way I expected my family to preserve the old Italian ways. In that freeze frame: We are crowded in a cellar. The voices are loud and speaking Sicilian dialects or broken English. The clothes are dark, modest fabrics, not yet light and pastel. The long tables are laden with lasagna or pastaciut', stuffed scungili (octopus), breaded cardoons, eggplant, *finucc'* (fennel), thick squares of Sicilian pizza, red wine in squat glasses, and such. The men are gathered around each other shouting and tossing fingers into a circle, playing a game I only know as *cinque bits*. The women are

173

equally expressive, not infrequently on some scandalous American-style behavior, such as permissive parents or *divorce*. We kids are clamoring for our turn to pin the tail on the donkey. If it's holiday time, Uncle Valentino has gathered us kids, a dozen crawling on one couch, leading us in Christmas carols, as we try to outdo each other. When it's late and everyone is sleepy, I hear, "Cusumanos, fall in line, single file," my father's boisterous military command. We don't even think of not obeying. We know what is next: He makes us sing that family song he wrote, *We are the Cusumanos*.

This summer day I look around bemused at my couch-potato or flabby Italian-American relatives who have not wandered far from the New Jersey/Connecticut suburbs. Most Italians are famously rooted to place and immovable, staying put for generations. My siblings and I, members of our own brand of diaspora, propelled by an anxiety instilled in us early on, exhibit a certain leanness and muscularity. Anxiousness and eagerness have scattered us, eventually around the world, and the perpetual movement that sheds pounds, or at least tones that muscle that runs though us, seems to be what neutralizes those states. We parlay our worries into incessant activity, considered by some as positive addictions, by others a compulsion. My brother, Tom, and I have just done our third or fourth Donner Lake Triathlon together, and Tom will do dozens more triathlons, never relaxing his training. For me, triathlons are kinder, gentler than the two marathons and dozen half-marathons I have run. You could say I've slowed down. But the muscle twitches.

A few years ago I met Dan, whose family is third-generation Californian, with places named after them. Our relationship endures some challenges, but movement is a sort of glue. He has instilled my love of the Sierra Nevada Mountain range where his family took him as a child. We backpack there, sometimes with Chuck leading the charge. We have trekked in New Zealand over the Routeburn and Rees-Dart tracks. Then over Southeast Alaska's Chilkoot Pass, in rain with Chuck and his two sons, Chuckie and Michael (the latter of whom will opt out of our sort of movement and become an expat chef in Italy where he'll raise a family). One night, I lured my entire family up a mountain in Northern California. They came, they saw, they marveled. I made sure what we ate was, not *merican'*, but bona fide *Italiano*—spaghetti and meatballs—and packed with energy restoring carbs and other goodness for our mutual muscle.

13

My Whole Tam Family, 1991

Mount Tamalpais in Marin County just north of San Francisco is not really a mountain, but a ridge trending east to west, bending north upon itself, like a punctuation mark, into what is called Bolinas Ridge. Tam undulates, like a three-breasted maiden in repose—its three designated "peaks" are West, Middle, and East, this last, the highest. Ridge or mountain, Tam's rumples, folds, and warps feature some of the most appealing landscape, from grassy knolls and meadows to oak woodlands and redwood forests. Canyons, falls, and cataracts score the sensitive watershed in Marin County, just north of San Francisco. Wildflowers proliferate, raptors sail the sky, waterfowl streak the lakes, an occasional mountain lion stalks prey here. Hikers are about as likely to encounter mule deer as other humans. Anyone who travels California's Interstate 101 north of the Golden Gate Bridge sees Tam's legendary sleeping maiden profile on the western sky. Though unassuming in stature—her highest point is only 2,571 feet—the maiden sprawls fingers, flanks, feet, and toes into the backyards of encircling Marin and is loved for her wilds that weave so skillfully with residential areas.

Its West peak interests me most this year. From there, in startling abundance are heavenly vistas that encompass

San Francisco, the East Bay's Mount Diablo, and twenty-six miles off-coast to the Pacific's Farallon Islands. You have not seen fog until you've watched it gather at Tam's feet, mount its peaceful takeover of the mountain, then retreat. From the summit, it looks like a monster tidal wave washing up over hill after hill then back in slow mo. It's a spectacle I imagine has been taking place forever, before Francis Drake sailed the Gate, when California was still home to numerous thriving Native American tribes.

The fog is as mystical as Tam's name—whose origin has no consensus of expert opinion. Is it Spanish for "country of the Tamals" (a Native American group)? Or Coast Miwok for "bay country mountain?" Or some variation therein? Devotees won't quibble. It is simply The Mountain to which they take their boots or bikes—or big families. Poised at the edge of our continent, Tam has a few hundred miles of trails and fire roads winding up from sunny inland villages over peaks and down to Marin's misty seashore. There are the Cataract Trail, a riparian corridor rife in spring with the gorgeous fetid adders-tongue, western wood anemones, ferns, falls, and redwood shade; the Dipsea, its toes in the sea and head in the clouds, along which I've seen coralroot orchids; Steep Ravine, with vistas and forest overgrown with bracken, sword and maidenhair ferns, moss-covered logs and stumps, and a boulder-choked ravine. Around Bon Tempe and Lagunitas lakes, I've seen coots, ducks, cormorants, a great blue heron.

There is on Tam's West peak an old historic inn with several detached cabins built in 1904, a guarded secret by those who know the complex well. The West Point Inn was once served by a railroad that chugged out of Mill Valley or Stinson Beach (formerly called Willow Camp), where well-heeled people arrived on horse-drawn stagecoach to meet the train. Today hikers or bikers reach the inn along the Matt Davis Trail or the Old Railroad Grade, now a fire road.

The inn consists of a main lodge with several very small bedrooms, the spacious downstairs with living and dining room, and a good size wrap-around deck, from which to watch the nocturnal heavens or the morning fog. It has no electricity (propane lights only), just some solar-and-wind-powered batteries for a couple of refrigerators. The kitchen is equipped with a large stove and utensils for guests to cook their meals. Five detached cabins, each with three to four beds, are scattered along the ridge looking down on San Francisco, 1,750 feet below.

I drop my voice to a whisper because in 1988 I put my hand over my heart and swore not to write about the inn. I first stayed at the inn during an outing with a group of ten women, all of us travel writers. We hiked the Matt Davis Trail and rested at the amazing outdoor amphitheater, 4,000 stones of open-air amphitheater laid in the 1930s by the Civilian Conservation Corps. Almost every summer since 1913 theater-goers have flocked to a play at this Mountain Theatre. *Abraham and Isaac*, a miracle play, and Malvolio's scenes from *Twelfth Night* marked the theatre's 1913 debut.

A short jaunt from the theater along a manzanita ridge took our troupe to the stone and wood inn. We were met and gathered together by then-innkeeper Daniel Meyerowitz in the living room with its large romantic stone fireplace and rocking chairs. Daniel asked each one of us to promise we would not write about the inn. Even though it is against all best journalistic standards to do so, none of us balked. We all knew the power of our stories to send droves of tourists to a place after we had written about it. I hereby declare a three-year statute of limitations on that promise.

Now I can tell you, from my high vantage that first night, looking out to sparkling light-studded nights and in the early morning gasping at the way prongs of earth or manmade structures pierced the thick quilt of fog I decided I would have my entire family stay here. Oh yes, I would indeed. Mount Tam became a metaphor for heaven, the place I had since first grade planned to take my whole family on Judgment Day.

First I had to become a member of the nonprofit West Point Inn Association helping at work parties to repair its ancient floor, polish its pressed tin wainscoting, and otherwise help with upkeep. I was thus eligible to host overnights at the inn.

Three years later, I joke with my sister Lisa who lives in Annapolis, "Our family has become a national chain with outlets in San Francisco, Los Angeles, New York, and other major metropolitan areas. Reunions used to be easy as pizza pie when we were just a Mom-and-Pop operation." Lisa laughs and I know that we both long for something we didn't know we had growing up.

It is 1991, the year of our parents' Golden Anniversary. July is a good month for all to travel to our family reunions, but no easy feat with us scattered far and wide. It has taken the better part of the whole year preceding our gala event, to plan the celebrations for (headcount over fifty, I'm guestimating), to get everyone committed to the time frame, for Chuck and Jim to donate plane fares to some of the younger struggling siblings with little kids. Whew, it's like running a small country trying to correspond back and forth (in case, you forget, there is no widespread use of email or cell phones this year).

Jim and his wife Jane, who live in Los Altos, and I do most of the planning since the celebration is in our neck of the woods. The long weekend includes a pizza date for just the ten siblings who will reminisce about growing up together, an afternoon barbecue and volleyball match for the whole tribe, a vow renewal ceremony for Mom and Dad at Saints Peter and Paul Church in North Beach, and a reception at Il Fornaio in Palo Alto. I convince Jim and Jane to have us all spend the night at the West Point Inn on the Saturday evening.

Everyone flies in on schedule and our homes bulge with sprawled bodies like old times. Friday night, my sisters, Grace, Terry, Lisa, Tina, Donna, and I arrive in Sausalito for the pizza powwow. We have time to kill so we wander up a long thin staircase of a boutique on Bridgeway labeled Wet Dreams, a sexual pleasure shop. Donna who loves curios buys condoms in a walnut shell. They are pink and ridged we find out later. As we file out to cross the street to Caffe Trieste, a man is poised in cowboy stance videotaping us. The man turns into our brother Salvatore. "We thought it was an ice cream place," says Donna.

The pizza parlor is in the back of venerable Trieste in a private room just big enough for ten of us. As we feast on crusty pies and drink red wine in squat goblets, I tell my brothers and sisters how I once took Mom and Dad to the original Trieste in San Francisco's North Beach on a Saturday afternoon when the opera singing owners entertained us. Mom and Dad loved it and were transported back to Peterstown, the Italian enclave in Elizabeth, New Jersey, where their immigrant parents and others from Italy settled in the early 1900s.

It's actually a first (and a last) for the ten of us to be together, alone with each other. What to do? We play a trivia game that transports us back more than two decades to Rahway, where we spent most of our formative years. We name the city parks—Squire Island and Wheatena—and the factories—Merck, which had explosions, usually in summer, Birdsall, which made heating equipment, Esso, which spewed fumes in the area. No one can recall the name of the plastics one that made hula hoops, but

Grace and I tell how we gathered melted colored plastic from its trash, conceptual artwork.

We describe facts about our quiet neighbors on maple-tree lined Price Street where we grew up.

Who carried a black lunch box to work every day?
Who had an aviary in back?
Who taught school?
Who gave three of us ladders one summer to pick his cherries?
Who had the club foot?

We yell at the same time the answers—*Mr. Mueller, the Adamses, Mr. Youngblood, Mr. Osborne, Billie Claddock.* We recall the complainers, Mr. Pittenger who came out in his guinea T (our word) and was scary. The meanie prize went to Mrs. Lengel who may well have been the party who upturned our lawn statue of the Blessed Virgin Mary and who poured black shoe polish on one of Jim's friend's car. We never stop to consider what the neighbors might have thought and felt of the big Italian family that descended on the mostly WASP 'hood in 1955 and then got bigger with kid after kid popping out and filling the streets with more kid noises.

I'm pretty sure my siblings will love Mount Tam and the inn. I have sent out long letters and teased them with images of moonbeams through pine boughs and worked in some tricky image of the fog, how it rolls in like a benign tidal wave.

Although my father used to weave his dreams aloud of moving to the country, he is now 71 and stiffened from an old war wound (but soundly dry for nearly thirteen years). I know that my mother hates bees and all insects. Dirt and rodents like bats and squirrels don't thrill her. She generally has a distaste for the outdoors. My fantasy scenario diminished is by two.

Consumed with plans for the most important aspect—the food—I haven't given much thought to sleeping arrangements. The ratio of space to person is so favorable compared to our childhood days, who would complain? I prepare the feast—spaghetti and meatballs— the patent Last Supper for an Italian family on Judgment Day. My brother Tom's kids, Carmela, Tommy, Christina, and Antonio are used to my dragging them off on outdoorsy trips for my magazine assignments. So they don't mind helping me. We pack my hatchback Toyota with shopping bags full of cans of Italian tomatoes, pounds of ground chuck, links of Sicilian sausage, Parmagiano, spaghetti, biscotti, wine, coffee. Luckily, the inn is equipped with industrial-size pots, pans, and bowls for cooking up large quantities of sauce and mixing and frying dozens of meatballs and sausage for the tribe. The familiar aromas of garlic and hot olive oil are the perfume of good memories—or memories refined by time—like the one where Grace and I have to run home from school to "start the gravy and meatballs" for the family dinner.

I recognize the cooking and all the demanding preparation as an exercise in nostalgia. That is, nostalgia perfectly defined as "it ain't what it used to be." I never forget the bad days, the punishing ways of my father, his drinking "daze" and all the pecking-order discontent and rumbles. At the same time, I prefer to focus on something else that was happening that may only be seen from distant time.

I was masterful at cultivating my dislike of routine and of Rahway, of New Jersey—its seemingly endless gray color, its lack of big nature, which I could discover only in books, its utterly conforming residents. Yet something was nourishing me. It was the mysterious ground of blood ties. Of course, I didn't know it any more than a bird knows itself from its air, a fish from its water, a cow from its pasture. The continuity of ourselves with our place or habitat is undervalued.

Moving all over the country has certainly broadened us all in ways. My brothers, highly esteemed in their fields of business and science, climbed corporate ladders, fared well professionally and monetarily, and heeded the patriarchal exigency in my family to Make thy Father proud. My sisters, for chapter-length reasons, did not wander as far physically from the nest as my four brothers and I, the bookworm, who has found her much longed-for sentimental education in San Francisco.

But we have lost something, too, in our interrupting that feeding tube of place. The loss is summed up in the sweet recall of countless extended family gatherings of our youth with grandparents, aunts, uncles, cousins, and a steady flow of new arrivals from Sicily. During a feast, we sat in cellars on benches and unmatched chairs around several oblong tables unevenly linked, with linen tablecloths thrown over them. Dish after dish of Sicilian/American food and drink would appear in what today seems such lavish spreads—my grandmothers' thick pizza with anchovies, bread-and-herb-stuffed squid, vinegar-garlic chicken, olive-oil soaked greens, crusty breads, and lots of macaroni with cheeses, pastries, hardy red wine, and coffee. There would be loud talk, gestures, laughter, singing, gyrations as jokes were told, always great animation and occasionally even the Judgment-Day gnashing of teeth.

Now our honorable elders, the first generations of naturalized Americans, are dying off and the succeeding generations have, understandably though regrettably, put the corporate ladders before the home-style conviviality. It seems all but possible now to bring back those Mom-and-Pop days. And maybe we do not want to.

Maybe all we want is to act on the urge to get our family out into nature, an adult translation of a childhood fantasy. Faith and myth embed themselves in the emotions and psyche the way life's first seasons and early lessons do. And the wilderness, which long ago replaced my church-going, is an exercise in salvation. One has to leave almost everything behind to go into the backcountry and there is a Judgment-Day aura to each trip as you wander a path and wonder each time will you survive the odds of the outdoors, be damned or saved.

I know that the closest I will ever get to taking my whole family on any semblance of a backcountry outing is here atop Mount Tamalpais.

185

With the cooking underway on the six-burner stove, I stand at the top of the fire road and watch everyone arrive on my mountain. I greet each clutch of family like Saint Peter at the pearly gates. I couldn't feel grander this day if we were on land deeded to us, or staying in a stately mansion. This is much cooler—a publicly owned place I share privately with the ever-blossoming Cusumano family tree.

My first clue that I may have overlooked details comes when I see sister Terry round the final bend on the fire road. She is smiling (probably with relief) but flushed a deep red. The upward haul to this elevation in hot, dry air is not the flat sea-level ground of the Jersey Shore where she lives. Terry, an earth mother of five, who loves more than anything our being together, does not once complain.

Slowly I realize this fantasy of mine is not perfectly suited to all. The inn is maybe a bit too rustic. Even if they survive without carsickness the drive along the winding road leading to the parking area, the hike up the mountain is a strain. As someone whose very definition of luxury is *being in wilderness and not having to sleep in a tent,* I have overlooked the reactions of those who like fancy hotels. Fortunately, those people get into the spirit of the place and rather than complain just joke. There is feverish excitement as each new party arrived and hugs and jokes or sottovoce comments are exchanged. And soon enough we are all there.

The younger kids run up to the East Peak where little is left to reveal the wild days the summit had seen. I tell them how East Peak rocked with the Tavern, built at the turn of the century. The local gentry danced, dined, overnighted there, and furtively sipped spirits during Prohibition. The Tavern's decaying remains were burned away only in the 1950s. In their place now, a visitor center and fire lookout bear witness to no more frolicking. They climb the lookout tower that offers panoramic views of Tiburon, Sausalito, and San Francisco.

Although it is most often cool atop the mountain, this evening, maybe due to the breath of four dozen hot Sicilians, is like a muggy New Jersey summer night. We settle down with wine, cold drinks, and antipasto on the wraparound porch, then gather at long tables of unmatched heights, with unmatched chairs. When the main course is dished out, heads are bent over steaming mounds of spaghetti and there comes the one and only moment of silence that night. "Let's say grace," is repeated down the line of diners and on cue we recite the singsong prayer, which comes out like a Buddhist chant with no space between wors, *BlessusOLordand thesethygiftswhichweareabouttoreceive fromthybountythroughChristourLord.*
Amen.

My gratitude is that amid the chaos of distance and mobility, a sacred ground is always available sit upon together. A vision of us tightly seated at table and chairs on Price Street under smoke stacks morphs into this airy setting on top of a mountain. I wonder if all those early upper-crust Californians who came by rail to this place imagined that one day a boisterous, over-sized Sicilian family from New Jersey would crowd this porch, twirl spaghetti, spear meatballs.

It is late and dark as promised, a moon appears through the pine boughs near the porch and the Bay Area glows like footlights. We are on the stage, laughing and teasing and telling our same old repertoire of stories until late. Jim and Dan, Terry's husband, play the piano in the grand dining room and we sing loud, out of tune, in tune, and then push each other trying to get our eyes up to the inn's telescope to find stars and planets in the heavens. If any mountain lions or coyotes wander nearby they might wonder what manner of beasts go here.

Regarding the current sleeping arrangements, I haven't thought about how it has been a couple of decades since we last slept under the same roof and that we have gone on to bigger spaces, houses with plenty of bathrooms. Bathrooms, we have at the inn—five of them—just barely enough. But private beds or rooms we did not—everybody has to share cabins or rooms.

The younger kids who are to share a couple of the multi-bed cabins simply stay up to all hours of the night in the main lodge, crashing on the floor, couches, chairs. Married couples double up in the dorm-style cabins and the complaints and cracks about who farts, who snores, or who talks in whose sleep will come for days after. Notwithstanding being short on sleep, everyone is in good form by morning kibitzing again.

Chuck, a CFO in Southern California, stands on the porch, sipped his coffee and extends a thumb and index finger to frame a forested slope. He clears his voice to make a serious announcement, "Tom, Jim, what do you think? Condos there; the golf course there."

"How about a multiplex cinema?" suggests Tom.

"We'll probably have to put in another road," says Jim.

Someone suggested that the impossible view of San Francisco floating in a sea of fog is "spray painted" and another responds that such trompe l'oeil was more characteristic of Los Angelenos. Chuck, a Los Angeleno, begs to differ. Terry keeps exclaiming, "Really? No! Really? No!" and someone says, "Hey, Ter, want to buy the Golden Gate Bridge." Through her uncontrollable laughter she pokes fun at herself, "I can't—I already bought the Brooklyn!" The fog rolls in as it has since time immemorial. Slow and soundless and awesome.

Grace laughs and will always recall this day on Tam, sleeping in a bed where "my head was going out the window and we were above the clouds."

As my family chatters away and recounts the high and low points of their night of sleeping with the sound of animal noises and sleepers snoring and farting, I retreat with my coffee to sit cross-legged in silence before the slo mo takeover by fog. I had once seen a woman sitting in lotus on a hill above the road that leads up here, where it looks straight down on the Pacific. She was swaying her long hair and her upper body like a piece of seaweed on the ocean bottom. She and dozens of others were stopped in their tracks by a red sun slipping below a layer of fog-cloud packed as tight as cottage cheese curds over the ocean.

I stare out at the Transamerica Pyramid shooting its incisor top through the dense cloud over the city. I think of all the stories we have told and re-told in New Jersey, in California, wherever we gathered, how we have our share of disappointment, pain, suffering, but we are weaving a pretty decent family mythology. In two days, July 6, Mom and Dad will be married fifty years.

As it turns out, Father Anthony, the priest whom I have arranged to preside over their vow renewal (*Do you still take each other? As is?*), has been a parish priest in St. Anthony of Padua, Peterstown, New Jersey, where my parents exchanged wedding vows in 1941.

Shortly after this day, I will begin to write *The Tale of the Last Cannoli*, a novel about breaking the family curse by telling a new tale.

14

Dances With Marmots, 2008

In my middle years
I've become rather fond of the way.
Sometimes I go alone through the forest
to see things that only I can see.
I follow streams to the source
and sit and watch clouds come up.
Or perhaps I meet another [backpacker] and
we laugh and sing and I forget the way home.
Adapted from a poem by Wang Wei, 8th century
(Tang Dynasty) poet

With the exception of a couple of tango-related interruptions, I have now backpacked through some mountain wilderness every summer since 1992. This summer following a two-year hiatus due to my living in Argentina, Chuck and I resumed our annual trek. We set out late one July day on the John Muir Trail in our ritualistic silence, each absorbing the message of our great effort in her or his way.

As always backpacking is a meditative art just as tango is. Both can be summed up as "just walking." In backpacking, as in tango, you either find the walking to be a rich and infinitely deep experience. Or you are phenomenally bored, see only the bugs, dirt, and broken-rock trails, find the 40-pound weight on your back insufferable, find digging your own latrine vulgar and distasteful. Those averse to tango, similarly, find the inescapable intimacy with other frightening or a turn off.

However, it doesn't follow that every tango dancer will love backpacking—the skeeters were hell this year and it was hot and the way was difficult. Most tango dancers probably would wisely rather save their feet for the work of scuffing polished wood floors. But, like the poet, I am called to the forest, to the paths deep into wilderness, away from "tired, nerve-shaken, overly civilized" folks that John Muir noticed in populated parts. (I am befuddled by the latest scare-du-jour—that our birthrates, in Europe in particular, are falling dangerously low. I see no evidence—except at some milongas, maybe—that human beings, who are making a mess of the planet, will be in short supply anytime soon. Would that they were.)

Chuck and I met at Tuolumne Meadows and were on our way down Lyell Canyon on the ever-popular JMT. The Tuolumne River was very low as were all the many stream crossings (which would be no problem if there were fewer humans). Our first day was an easy initiation to the art of walking with our whole survival kit on your back. We did only five miles. But the second day—due to our mis-planning—we climbed way too many miles on feet and legs hardly broken in.

"Llamas," I kept bleating to Chuck's shadow. "Llaaa-maaaas. . .I told you we should've taken llamas." Actually, I hadn't. But as I studied the trail of ground dust and the footprints of many hikers before me many stories took shape in my wide open mind. My brother was always way ahead of me so I only came to know that I had taken the right turn at a junction by his distinct kidney-bean-shaped waffle prints, which I now know like the back of my sunburned hands.

On day two, we began our ascent of 12,235-foot Mount Lyell, Donahue Pass, in good form. But there was so much up, up and then down, down that we were in pathetic shape by mid-afternoon. Just as in tango, when the dance is not feeling as rapturous as I know it can, I did not blame the form. I didn't even blame the emptiness. I simply kept mindful of the moment, of my surroundings. I watched my breath. My knees, feet, and back muscles hurt. But the beauty of the scenery, which my photos barely capture, was never lost on me. I recited the names of a rainbow spectrum of wildflowers I saw, which have bloomed early this dry year, a litany of distraction from pain:

Mountain Heather; Wild Azalea; Columbine; snowy flax or phlox; rock flower; penstemon; Mariposa lilies; corn lily (or false hellebore); Johnny Jump-ups; asters; monkey flower; lupine; larkspur; tiger lilies; sierra arnica; mule's ears; cinquefoil; buttercups; groundsel; goldenrod; Indian paintbrush; owl's clover; swamp onion; shooting stars. Ommm. Ommm. Ommm. Oh my 'aching' twisted karma . . .

I hoarded my breath, sniffing in the aroma of lodgepole pines, white pines, red firs, as if I could carry it home and revel in it for another week. I watched their tree roots that became steps in the middle-earth. I studied the position of glacial erratics, reminders of the cataclysms that only recently quarried, scoured and shaped this landscape. I drank straight from high streams of snowmelt thinking how they all lead back to ONE—all branching streams of the snowpack in its granite keep.

As in tango, I thought often of my axis or balance. Any jarring turn of my head up or to the side would throw off my weight now distributed in an unfamiliar way—and I'd be like a flailing turtle when I fell (don't tell Chuck, but I fell twice when he wasn't looking). With my backpack laden with a bear canister, tent, sleeping bag, food, water and such, my center of gravity shifted from my third abdomenal chakra to my solar plexus, the crucial one in tango connection, and as in tango, I always flexed my knees—especially on the downhill. My trusty French Vasque hiking boots have to go now, though. They are too worn from many miles, many years. And they badly bruised my big toenails, the cumulative pounding equal to one swing of a sledge hammer per toe.

We camped in four beautiful spots—five miles up Lyell Canyon, in a high meadow just the far side of Donahue Pass, at Thousand Island Lake, and at Rosalie Lake. We found a lake or stream each day to soak away most of the dirt and some of the inevitable inflammation. This is the segment of the Sierra backbone that inspired Muir's moniker, Range of Light, due to ubiquitous light-reflecting waters, rushing or still. Unlike previous trips, we saw no bears, but Chuck let a marmot get my sesame sticks one day—my favorite day food in the backcountry. Oh, but I made that marmot's fur stand on end, tapping my walking stick against the rock crevice where he thought he was hiding from me, that varmint. "You get your tail out here right now, marmot, you hear me? I'm going to tan your hide . . . " Tap, tap, tap. I dressed him down to no avail. Other yellow-bellied marmots (*Marmota flaviventris*) were just as brash but thereafter I kept my own eye on my victuals.

We came out of the woods on Sunday early, exiting at Devils Postpile National Monument on the east side of the Sierra, amid overly civilized (albeit very clean-smelling) day trippers, the sound of cellulars piercing the silence. We had been immersed in the rapture of the wilderness, five days worth, so it was jarring at first. We got long hot showers at the ski lodge at Mammoth and were once again one of them.

I never rush back to the city so I spent the night at Lee Vining (Mammoth Lakes felt too overrun with the nerve-shaken), a city to love for its location fairly on the banks of the big blue Mono Lake with its crunchy pillars of tufa (same root as taffy?). LV had many French tourists and I loved listening to them speak, a foil for the vernacular of a lot of tatooed bikers. The latter are no longer intimidating—as they were in my youth back in chemical Rahway, NJ. I sat next to a couple of them at Bodie Mike's, the ribs place in town—and eavesdropped on their very low-key conversation. BTW, the food at Bodie Mike's is decent for being what it is, not fancy, just meat and potatoes. The salad bar—iceberg lettuce style—was welcome fresh fare after five days of dried foods.

The next day I was up before dawn, so attuned to breaking camp early. I strolled a trail at the Mono Lake Visitor Center until the red desert sun poked above Mono Lake turning the salty water and tufa taffy pink. Travel Tip: Make your own French roast coffee in your Lake View Motel room, then carry it over to the Garden House Coffee spot next door; sit outside near the scorching rows of dahlias and other terraced flowers and plants. This is a great meditative spot. The coffee is too weak and tasteless, but the baked goods—I had a bear claw—are fresh and good. It's at 30 Main Street, Lee Vining (tel: 760-647-6266). Oh, don't let that one loud cell talker screaming chitchat to someone in L.A. diminish the setting.

Back in San Francisco my blackened toes stopped hurting after a couple of days and to my surprise I could soon step into my tango heels without any pain—good feet genes. So I danced at a lovely new milonga—Olivia and Jonathan's at Four Points Sheraton in San Rafael. It was quite enjoyable dancing under the twilight sky on a decent floor.

On Saturday, I attended the Dharma Talk at San Francisco Zen Center, the grassy smell of tatami mats my virtual route back to wilderness. Shosan Victoria Austin, one of my teachers over the past twenty years, told some engaging stories of the Buddha—Siddhartha Gautama—and his entering into enlightenment, or liberation, which I like to call it these days. Before he became Buddha or Awakened One, Siddhartha recalled a moment of unprecedented equanimity experienced in nature as a child. So he sat down under a bodhi tree and discovered it again. And a world religion was born. That simple. Nature, wilderness, tatami mats, wooden dance floors— the good news is that equanimity, liberation, rapture are always at hand. Vickie recited the above poem by Wang Wei (which I at first mis-heard as One Way). It so well suited how I feel—about backpacking, tango, and life. When I forget my way back home, it means I forget to pick up the bones of suffering, of aversion or craving, of prefab idea. And I slip my feet painlessly onto the earth where they are, just laugh and enjoy the dance, no matter how far it may be from what I think the path should be.

15

Deadman Canyon,
Another Fine Mess, 1996

Sometimes when I'm backpacking with Chuck, I feel like Bob Hope and Bing Crosby in one of those On the Road to Somewhere movies. "Beats taking the bus," says Hope to Crosby as they escape the bad guys on a camel in the Moroccan desert. Our own screwball humor distracts from the physical discomfort and pondering why we do what we do.

We are hiking the Deadman Canyon loop with Dan. We all meet up at the ranger station to pick up our wilderness permit in Sequoia National Park.

"Do you know what to do about food and bears?" queries the ranger.

"Put a sign on it DO NOT EAT," says Chuck.

"In Spanish and English," says Dan.

"In case of migrant bears," say I.

The ranger patiently abides our *schtick*. That trip goes off smoothly, without incident to report, as if Dan is the incident-neutralizing factor.

This time, a semi-comedy of errors, it was just Chuck and I whose motto might have been Hope's USO pun, "Where there's death, there's Hope." Omens foreshadowed us from the start. The broad glacier-carved valley we would hike through was aptly called Deadman

Canyon. The name comes from the Iberian sheepherder who died and was buried here. He was either murdered or died of illness, history is uncertain, and his death occurred some time in the late 1800s.

This year, a **MISSING** sign was posted everywhere, from the visitor centers to trees along the backcountry trail. An experienced park ranger had been missing for a few weeks after he left on a lone trip into the backcountry of Sequoia Kings Canyon National Park. The unofficial report was that he was presumed dead, probably having suffered a fatal fall. Falls, along with hypothermia, are the most common causes of death in this wilderness.

We had headed out of the Lodgepole area of Sequoia National Park one morning. At the Twin Lakes turn-off, we took the detour that for some reason no one else was taking to Rowell Meadow. Well we got away from the crowds all right and we figured out why. Rowell Meadow is just outside the national park boundary. It is forest service (land of multiple uses, or abuses, depending on your view), so Rowell was a pasturing area for cattle. It was very eaten up by grazing and strewn with numerous old and fresh cow pucks. The only water was low in a stream the color of dung. But we had to drink or die and cook, so we filtered it and tripled our iodine treatment. Cowbells serenaded us through the night. At least we didn't have to worry about bears, one small consolation. Rowell Meadow was our first mistake on that trip.

On the second day out, having survived stinky Rowell Meadow, we were up early and in good form to beat the heat. On the trail after an hour or so, we stopped to that Chuck could climb up onto the granite ridge behind us to take a picture of the view. I rested and waited. I ate a snack, waited. I rearranged my backpack so the weight would not cause bunions on my hipbones. I waited.

I had waited close to thirty minutes for Chuck to return before I began to wonder. Finally, I decided I'd go see what kind of photos he was shooting with a point and shoot that took so long. I wrote the first of three notes that I have saved in a file since that episodic trip. I tore a sheet of paper out of my pocket-size journal that I always bring on backpack trips. In large block letters: WENT TO LOOK FOR YOU. C. 10:33 am. I placed the note right on top of my pack leaning against a rock and scrambled up the steep slope.

No Chuck in sight. On the off chance that he came down a different way from how I went up, he would see my pack and know I hadn't continued on the trail without him. I circled around the plateau but it produced no sign of Chuck. I noted the view of distant peaks that he had probably photographed. It was a million dollar view that no camera could do justice but it would make good show and tell for his wife. I noted the ledge with a drop, and thought it was not too precipitous. OK, I thought to myself, he's gone down another way and is waiting back at my pack. I climbed down and the note and pack was just as I left it.

I felt my first pang of anxiety. I waited and waited. The air was still. It would be a very hot day. I relished the fragrant air but against my better wishes, anxiety blossomed into full-fledged panic. The awful truth began to sink in. Deadman's Canyon, the missing backwoodsman. The prognosis did not bode well for me. My brother, in his typical trail haste had fallen into some abyss and was now lying dead or nearly dead.

Shaking with disbelief, I write a second note: *10:48 a.m. S.O.S. HELP – I LOST MY BROTHER UP THIS SLOPE/HELP. I'M LOOKING.*

I draw an arrow pointing up to where I was climbing and leave the note on my pack again. Up the slope I walk on wobbly knees, circling all over the granite table and yelling, *Chuck!* my voice cracking. Squirrels and mountain chickadees ignore me. *Why won't a ranger or another hiker come by?* I ask no one in particular. It is an early Saturday morning is why. Most sensible folks are not yet in motion. Chuck has us up at the crack of dawn and if I'm not ready when he is, he paces the camp site like a caged animal. Now look what happens.

Back down at my pack, no sign of anyone having come by. That's it. I have to take action. I write my final note: *11:10 am. – I'm walking to Grant Grove for help! EMERGENCY.* I know there was a fire road nearby that leads in a few miles to Grant Grove where there is a ranger station. To go quickly, I have to leave my pack. I start back, thinking how we'd need a helicopter to look for the body. This is the state I am in. I'm plagued with anguish, how Cheri, Chuck's wife, is going to be so disappointed and upset. How to tell her—*Chuck fell, maybe to his death. I can't find him.*

I can't believe it. Second day of our trip!

As I head to Grant Grove, a eulogy begins to spin itself through my mind. *He was the best brother a person ever had.* Good start. *He worked his butt off at Paul's Soda Shop, long, long hours and he turned his whole paycheck over to his parents to help them feed ten kids.* Not bad. *He fought well for his country in Nam.* I hadn't gotten even partly through his job and family history when a voice of sanity told me to turn back, this is ridiculous to leave the scene and my pack, which could draw bears and get me a fine.

Wait. It seems impossible, but there has to be the possibility that we missed each other. I meditate on an action. An answer comes, *Go to Comanche Meadow* (our next stop for the day). I have my doubts but at least I can find someone there and ask for help. I head back to my pack, stash the notes, start hiking and yelling his name, which feels really silly in the woods. Some twenty minutes into the hike I hear an answer. Here comes Chuck around the bend.

"Where'd you go?"

"No, where'd you go?"

"I came back in less than ten minutes. You were gone."

"I never moved . . . well except after thirty minutes to go look for your corpse."

"Hmmm . . . guess we missed each other. I thought you had gone on. But realized after twenty minutes you couldn't be that far ahead."

"Yeah, yeah, go take a hike."

"I am. We are." Crosby and Hope on the road to nowhere.

We lost at least an hour and the whole imbroglio added that much more fatigue. By the time we reached first day's layover, Comanche Meadow, we were pretty tired. Too tired to even argue whose fault the snafu was.

The trip went on less eventful and even with rewards that helped us bond rather than bicker—for the most part. For example, the next day's site, Roaring River, was the most beautiful campsite. It was furnished with a granite "kitchen" (the perfect flat rock with space) and "dining room furniture"—a sawed log table, a cook's seat for watching the food as it cooks, "guest seats" in the fireplace area should company stop by—smooth logs and cut ones. Plus extra tent area, nice and flat. It was kept so well by the ranger who lives in his ranger hut there.

We knocked on the ranger's door to ask if there was a food storage box at the next site up near the pass. The ranger was cooking soup for himself and very friendly. No, he said. We asked about the bear activity. Not too much because it is above treeline. You never know though. I felt like we always got the same response from the rangers. And then, I must have said my wisdom about sleeping with your food in the tent above treeline. The ranger said absolutely not, never.

Chuck, who respects authority more than I do said, "See, I told you." Back at our site, I said, "Oh he's just giving us the party line because he works for a government agency and he can't wink and say do as you like. I told Chuck that I knew for a fact that there were rangers who slept with food in their tent and I have read reputable guidebooks where the author said he does it in certain areas—like above treeline. And so it goes, our ongoing opposing views on bears and food.

We arose leisurely the next morning and had a breakfast of coffee and maple brown sugar oatmeal. I did a partial swim in the Roaring River when the sun hit it. We got started at about 10:45 a.m., which is very late for us, but understandable given the mental exhaustion from the day before. We headed up Deadman Canyon, which has got to be one of the most splendid canyons in the Sierra. It is beautifully carved, the walls in that soft open U shape. We passed a lot of cottonwoods along the creek and got to Lower Ranger Meadow at about 2:45 p.m. and took a break. Then on to Upper Ranger Meadow at about 3:30. We found our site. It was great. I loved it. It was also furnished with seats and a table for the stove and a good log lean-to for our packs. It reflected the handprint of our ranger back at Roaring River in its civility and décor. Winter was on the wind, I noted. Vegetation was brown. The mountain fall had browned the swamp onion, huckleberry, gooseberry, arnica, corn lily. There were pools in the granite in indentations like big grinding stones, on a slope the water running down and the sun hit it right so we could soak and dry off.

We hung the food from a tree, but there were really no trees tall enough for the bear system. Hanging our smelly shirts (bears don't really like our smell) over the food, we hoped for the best.

The next evening's campsite was at the foot of the pass. The site was above treeline so there was no place to hang our food. Chuck positioned his in the portable food storage container that bear's supposedly can't open, away from his tent. He didn't ask what I did with mine so I didn't have to lie. I slept snuggly with it wrapped inside my camp pillow. It was one good peaceful night before the big pass climb. And there would be several more trips together in the wilderness before the bear incident that foiled my coffee habit (see How Bears Take Their Coffee.)

With the high and difficult Elizabeth, over 11,000 feet in front of us we left camp early, on the trail with gear and all by 7:15 a.m. We made the summit at 10:20 a.m., not too bad. It was a difficult, beautiful climb with the granite swirling up with intermittent vegetation, those granite depressions that cup turquoise snowmelt.

We rested a little at the summit and then we started down the pass, with Chuck in the lead as always. I noticed that the trail got swampy here and there and sometimes it seemed the trail was a stream. I was trusting my Leader, not using my third eye to orienteer.

My Leader had lost the trail with me in tow. (To this day he'll say he didn't.) We were way off the trail. I wanted to turn around, even though it meant going up again and losing ground. No, no, said the Leader, we'll find the trail if we keep going down, which often is the case but not that time. We were getting farther and farther from the trail and then what happened was the vegetation was getting higher, so that we couldn't see what we were doing and we were running into thickets of Manzanita, thorny bushes, and uncooperative boulders with sudden drops. I was getting panicky and nervous again. Chuck was feigning calm at first. No sweat. Then I saw that he was nervous. We came to a spot where the only way to go was down a 10 to 15 foot ledge. It was steep and sheer and I knew we were sure to fall off a cliff and be like that lost ranger and die or die a slow death of exposure. Chuck had his GPS, but that only tells you where you are, not how to get out if you don't know the landform. We had close to 2,000 feet in elevation to lose to get down off the pass into the valley below.

We started bushwhacking blindly through willow and chaparral shrub. Beyond the hedgerows we looked straight down into the chasm, the hungry maw that was salivating, ready to swallow us. Scrambling through bushes, not knowing where the bottom may drop out was torture. Chuck scraped his Vietnam-injured hand, his bloody stubs briefly making me feel worse for him than for me, wondering if an old war wound brings back a bad memory. (However, Chuck has never publicly worn a shred of old war stress the way our father spectacularly did. When I'm feeling safer on terra firma I'll even tell you more about his overly Mr. Nice Guy persona. Right now, arrggghhh, damn brother of mine.)

"Another fine mess you've gotten us into," I said, as we stood on a steep ledge unable to go up or down.

"All we have to do is keep going down," Chuck dismissed my concern.

"No s–it, Sherlock. Easy for you to say," I said. Now there was no chance to go back up and find the trail. We tossed our heavy packs down in front of us, and then shimmied down ten, fifteen feet of rock, with the help of tree branches and each other's hands. We were scraped and bruised and very nervous. Not fun. We could at any point in the three to four thousand foot drop end up in a deadly "box" canyon, unable to go up or down and be forced to wait until we died or were rescued by concerned relatives. Missing signs with our faces would be posted all over the Sierra.

Eventually the vertical land smoothed out to a riverbed and I tested the impossible hypothesis that we were down. We. Were. Down.

Miraculously, two hours after we lost the trail, we had made it into the next valley, bruised, scraped, nerve-shaken. Chuck had the chutzpah to inform me, "I'd have turned back if Chuckie (his then-teen son) had been with us." *Ma putana fa Napoli*, as Grandma Catalano would have said. Never a dull moment with you, Chuck. But of course, true to form, he told Cheri, "Oh, we were never lost, I was never worried."

This trip started with my insisting Chuck not get ahead of me at Elizabeth Pass.

16

The Big Night—in Sicily, 2000

Wound a Sicilian, pay through the mouth

My sister Grace—who, I must have told you, is my junior by a year and four days—and I were once each other's shadow. We answered to each other's name, covered for each other's "crimes," and generally practiced *omerta*—before we could even pronounce this Sicilian word for the code of silence. Then things changed. Grace took a husband, a big house, and had kids. I took to the road in search of myself.

A few years ago, my sister, who never shared my desperate need to escape New Jersey, expressed interest in accompanying me on my world travels. I suggested she join me on a trip to Sicily, home to our forebears, during which I planned to lodge in hermitages open to lay travelers.

She jumped at the chance. By the time we reached Catania, the province dominated by the active volcano, Mount Etna, it was apparent how we were set in our ways. Grace enjoyed sleeping late, while I was up early. She liked lots of cappuccino stops, I liked to keep moving. She wanted shopping and beach sitting but I insisted on the pursuit of monastic settings.

The one exception to our contrasting time management was food. We are practically clones on this subject. We were bred in the soulful necessity of a well-composed feast. Our Sicilian grandparents put forth even the humblest meal—crusty bread, sweet butter, and wine, say—with the same reverence a priest bestows upon Holy Communion. Food wasn't just sacred. It was good. We were fed greens like chard, broccoli rabe, dandelions, and cardoons, cooked right from our grandparents' gardens. Pasta (we called it macaroni) was often hand rolled and we ate mounds of it, prepared in numerous ways, long before it was fashionable in America.

With hunger pangs uniting us one evening after a day with a few speed bumps, we arrived at Acireale. The baroque town sits on a sloping haunch of the moody firepit, Etna, over the Ionian Sea. We would spend the night in the eighteenth-century Franciscan monastery, San Biagio, amid cloisters, frescoes, lush gardens, statuary, and three ostriches.

On our way out for dinner, we passed a coarse-robed friar strolling the long halls. He jangled his ring of skeleton keys, reminding us that our lodging had a curfew. Still, we had plenty of time to savor a long, slow dinner Sicilian style. We ambled down the narrow back streets to the main thoroughfare, Via Vittorio Emanuele II, scrutinizing each and every restaurant. We were looking for signs—unpretentious lighting, paper tablecloths, men wearing bibs to guard against red splashes, dented metal pots on a hot stove, a plump grandmotherly type chanting a few bars of the melodious dialect, *Ven aca, sedi, mangia* (come here, sit, eat!).

With its cuisine (like its liturgy) founded on three farm products—wheat, olive, and grape—Sicily doesn't lack for tempting menus. But we had eaten a mediocre made-for-tourists meal the night before in Cefalu. I had ordered, assiduously in Italian, the *pulpo* (octopus), remembering my grandmother's delicious version stuffed with bread crumbs, cheese, and herbs and steeped in tomato broth. Sadly, the vulcanized fiber laid before us was better suited to the soles of a shoe. We were determined not to repeat the experience.

We finally settled on Oste Scuro at Piazza Lionardo Vigo. It was not quite the snapshot of our grandparents' kitchens, but its al fresco terrace across from a floodlit cathedral was warm and inviting. We watched two handsome, well-heeled couples step from a shiny black limousine and vanish laughing into the shadowy interior of the restaurant. They exuded a certain snob appeal mixed with sensuousness.

As our eyes followed them, I asked Grace, "What do you think, promising?"

"Let's give it a try," she said. I agreed, noticing that most patrons seemed to be Italian, not the Anglo tourists notorious for their lack of discriminating taste. I told the maitre d' in my best Italian—cobbled together from college courses and remembrance of words passed between Mom and Dad—that we wanted only to eat well, not like tourists as we had in Cefalu.

I began to expound on the previous night's rubbery octopus but trailed off as I saw his face flush deeply, his eyes dart in the sign of the cross, his nostrils flare. What had I said?

I was raised in an expressive culture. My own mercurial father could display passion, anger, disappointment, tenderness with a mere glance and my sister and I translated his meaning the way a blind person reads Braille, or a fisherman the sea.

My complaining had vexed the man, stirring up animosity for us implacable tourists. Perhaps we should leave, I thought. But he took a deep breath and with a dignified and ceremonial flourish he ushered us to a table. "Sit," he ordered tersely. We obeyed like the dutiful girls we had once been in our traditional Sicilian family.

"What did you say?" whispered Grace who had not missed the surfeit of climate changes in his face.

"I know what I said," I told her, still wondering if we should just bolt, "I'm not sure what he *heard*."

Presently, the maitre d' returned with two other men, a waiter and one dressed smartly in a suit. They had obviously been clued in that we were complainers. Our longed-for repast would be foiled again.

A carafe of red wine was set before us. After allowing us to briefly study the extensive menu, the three concluded that we should let them feed us. Their imperious tone told us not to object. A side serving table was set up next to ours. This lovely weekend evening had brought many diners to the popular Oste Scuro. Yet none seemed to be getting the excessive attention we were receiving.

Oste Scuro's menu featured at least 20 different antipasti, representing every flavor of Sicily that has seduced discriminating palates since a Sicilian, Archestrato from Gela, wrote the first cookbook, *The Sweet Taste*, 400 years before Christ. Grace and I were served in slow procession tangy-sweet caponata, platters of fried eggplant, fresh, creamy ricotta, buffalo-milk mozzarella, prosciutto; citrus and onion salad; broccoli rabe and wild fennel redolent of garlic and olive oil; conch tender as a first kiss; fire-roasted peppers. We took a few breaths and forked onto our plates *fritto misto* of artichokes and squid, frittata larded with pancetta, fresh fava beans, and peas, and roasted potatoes with caramelized garlic toes.

Every taste sensation between earth and sun, from the pungent to the sweet to the sour was laid upon our tongues. Generosity is nourishment in and of itself and we would have felt sated, even if these dishes had been less phenomenal. To our astonished delight, more *antipasti* were set before us—marinated porcini, fresh sardines, mussels, shrimp, and sautéed calamari. We worked the goodness from each morsel like bees sucking nectar from flowers.

As the parade of dishes crowded the serving table near us I learned that the smartly dressed man regaling us was none other than Oste Scuro owner Carmelo Muscolino who has run the establishment for more than thirty years. The pride Muscolino takes in his country's cooking was evidenced in these time-honored ingredients, from the fruits of sea and earth to the piquant kiss of garlic, fragrant embrace of olive oil, and tingle of lemon.

"Don't look now," I said to Grace, "but one of the guys waiting on us is *il Padrone* himself, master of the house."

"I'll kiss his ring," said Grace, smacking her lips, "his food is fabulous."

"I'm afraid he'll kill the cook," I said, "if I tell him it's anything but."

Catania's specialties include the aromatic pasta Norma, a rigatoni with tomatoes, fried eggplant, basil, and the sharp ricotta *salata*; pasta *cc'a muddica*, made with toasted bread crumbs, olive oil, and anchovies; pasta *cc'u trunzu*, with specially cultivated cabbage; and pasta *cc'u niuru*, mantled in a dark, sweet mix of squid ink and tomatoes. We were served Oste Scuro's versions of each one, plentiful enough to feed six people. Grace and I looked at each other. We understood that to stop eating was tantamount to trampling the flag.

But with each delightful swallow, my eyes bulged. My waistline felt no more distinct than the middle of a bell pepper. The taste of the food and the sheer abundance transported me back to my childhood when not one of our parents' ten children dared leave the table before cleaning their plates.

"Take small portions and eat very slowly," I advised Grace.

"Easy for you to say," she said, noticing that I would offer to serve her first, then fill her plate with more food than I took. I pushed the thought of the bill away. It loomed like an unreal dénouement in a Fellini film.

I began to understand how my cavalier criticism had desecrated these Sicilians' cherished patrimony. That they were ashamed of their compatriot who had fed us so poorly that I had felt compelled to broadcast it. The abundance and diversity of food served us—with nary a hint of fawning—was an implicit gag order. We accepted the "penance" for my blasphemy.

The four *paste* were delicious, perfectly *al dente* and balanced in the pairing of chewy and tender textures and of flavors—sweet, salty, robust, mild, aromatic. Each attested that the true genius of Sicilian cooking is in the use of honest, fresh ingredients mingled in imaginative ways. I wanted to convey my innate understanding of this ancient alchemy to our waiter, but he was not interested in small talk. He nodded to the maitre d' who came by, smiled, and asked, "How is everything?"

"Extraordinary! Superb!" we assured him too eagerly.

"*Bene*," he said and told us to follow him. We stood, not without difficulty, and followed him inside the restaurant where we all leaned over a case of silver and iridescent fish on ice. He asked us to choose which we wanted and when he saw the clouded look on our faces, he pointed to a four-to-five-pound red snapper and asked, "Will this one do?"

"There's more?" asked Grace, panicky.

"Uhh . . . *si* . . . of course . . ." I answered wistfully. I'd never been humbled by food in quite this way.

"How would you like it?" he asked.

"*To go*, tell him," said my sister who was on her first trip abroad. How to explain to her, whose mores have been steadfastly shaped in north Jersey, that she was no longer in Hoboken. I felt her eyes egging me to request that doggie bag.

"*Grigliata?*" he asked.

"*Sì, sì*," I mumbled. Grilled snapper it would be.

Back in our seats, I felt like a character in Jean Genet's theatre of the absurd, uncertain of which side of the playwright's master-slave equation we represented. We sipped wine to revive our long-gone appetites for the fish course and I refrained from telling Grace that *oste scuro* translated to "dark host." My thoughts grew even darker as I recalled that the thick menu included many types of *carne*, from rabbit and pork to veal scaloppini and famous Florentine *chianina* beef, all of which I ordinarily love.

The snapper arrived. Discreetly, I loosened my belt two notches. Grace grabbed the serving utensils and served me the larger portion. "Hey, look!" I exclaimed, "over there, that handsome man is staring at you!" I shoveled food from my plate back into hers as she turned. Of course, she didn't fall for that old gag but the comic relief was welcome—even if it hurt to laugh. We were drunk, not on wine, but on food.

The snapper was meltingly sweet and moist and we washed it down with more goblets of the rugged Catanese wine. Another platter arrived. It contained beautiful fresh fruit, including loquats, the sweet white-fleshed

Mediterranean fruit that would be criminal to pass up in Sicily. Just as I expelled the last of their mahogany pits, three different pastries appeared. I had always admired the Arabs' legacy to Sicily—an inventive finessing of almonds, pistachios, chocolate, sugar, eggs, and ricotta into an array of delectable *dolci*—until that moment. But we worked through the meal's crowning opulence like the actors with their death wish in *La Grande Bouffe*, even as the waiter posited a surreal trio of liqueurs—*lemoncello, arancello,* and *cioccolato*—in front of us.

Tears filled our eyes and we pondered the existential question of whether we'd died and gone to heaven or hell. About the time the espresso arrived, we scared up the courage to ask our waiter to please bring a check—any check.

Ma, perche avete fretta?—What's the hurry?—he asked. You must try our gelato next. *E fatto in casa.*

'No, please! We love homemade gelato! Right, Grace?" I said, vaguely aware that my shrill tone belied my words. Grace wrung her hands. And then, in my desperation, I remembered some received wisdom, the one thing in Sicily that might trump their need to compensate their wounded pride—a woman's chaste reputation.

"Signor," I begged, standing to block the way of our "dark host" to the kitchen that held our torture and delight. "We are lodging at San Biagio. They lock the doors at midnight. It's quarter to twelve—we must get back—or we'll have to sleep in the streets."

216

My plea magically triggered the evening's anti-climactic climax. Our check arrived within minutes. It would be astronomical. We didn't care. Oh, we would pay anything for the pleasure of waddling away from that wonderful restaurant. But the full bill was only 158,000 lire, about $75 for two of us.

Ecstatic at the unexpectedly low total, I offered to treat Grace and pay the entire bill, which she accepted. It was a small price to pay for lessons learned on both our accounts. While I imparted a modicum of traveling etiquette to my younger sister (like there is no Italian word for "doggie bag"), we both learned that one must also be prepared for the dark host. He could be lurking just behind the next *prezzo fisso* menu. Next time, my sister and I will remember what to do: *Omerta.*

17

Brother, Can You Spare
Some Tent Space? 1999

Dad never tired of expressing his wishes, hopes, and dreams for his sons, that they be successful, college-educated, have good jobs, earn good money, have happy, fruitful marriages, and bear him lots of sons—*sons*, gender-specifically. In some form of poetic justice, all four of my brothers' firstborn were girls. (Thank-you, Goddess.) Dad got over it and loved all his grandkids, but "carrying on my name" by males never lost its currency with him. He had no special recommendation for his daughters (nor did Mom) who understood that Dad literally meant the cliché that women should be "barefoot in the summer, pregnant in the winter." Three of his daughters were married and pregnant by age 19, and a fourth eventually married her childhood sweetheart. Only Donna, the baby, and I, a middle kid, rewrote the prescribed formula.

From an early age I perceived that it was more interesting and attractive to be a boy in my family and so I identified with them on some level. I wouldn't call it penis envy—I enjoyed my so-called feminine side (clothes, nail polish, make-up, boys). But, for example, when Dad told me, I could go to college if I *really* wanted to—otherwise, I'd have to go to work and help support the family as

Terry had done before marrying—I did like the boys. I obtained a state scholarship, worked thirty some hours a week (and paid my parents room and board), and was the first girl in the long line of Cusumanos to obtain a college degree. That my parents came to my graduation ceremony from Kean University (then called Newark State) still astonishes me.

To this day, even though my rational brain knows there is no basis in reality, I have a sense of being taken more seriously when allowed to sit in on boys' stuff. So, on this summer day, even at my ripe, accomplished age, that old feeling is there when I am going to climb the highest peak in the Lower Forty-Eight, Mount Whitney, with not just one, but two of my big brothers, Chuck (third child, second son) and Jim (first child, first son,).

I'm excited that Jim, *Numero Uno*, asked me to drive and is willing to ride in my car, a 1986 Toyota Corolla hatchback, a gutless wonder. Since becoming an international who's who Silicon Valley chemist/entrepreneur, Jim has notably graduated from our penny-pinching Jersey days, and can afford the best of everything in cars, watches, clothes, homes, walking sticks. He generously tosses an expensive pair my way.

Jim is nine years older than me, kind of a surrogate father, the way Terry (seven years my senior), was a surrogate mother (I'd never have known about menstruation if I had to rely on Mom). My earliest memory of Jim is of his making monster faces that had me screaming *stop, stop*, and cutting off his index finger than screwing it back on, miraculously with no blood. He took all of us little kids for a ride in his vintage Lincoln Continental convertible that his bachelor godfather, Johnny Nash, gave him as a birthday gift. He traded it in for a red Pontiac convertible and had it painted with white pinstripes and I loved to watch him meticulously wax it in the sun.

Jim was from another planet, Mars. That's what he told his younger siblings and we believed him. He told his chums that too. Once he was riding bikes with a friend and told him how he came from Mars. The boy suddenly fell off his bike and Jim convinced him that he had made the fall happen. Jim wrote songs and drew comic strips— he was a natural artist but science was his deeper calling.

Jim played our old red upright piano and sang in rock bands that jammed in our cellar and had the next-door neighbor calling the cops. When he needed solitude he played piano alone in our cellar and the music drifted up and comforted everyone, as if it were a promise that Dad would never have another explosion. To this day the sound of piano induces a pleasant alpha state. Music was comfort to Dad too who once played French horn.

One summer day, when Jim was still a teenager, he had to lay off the piano. His devilish antics backfired. He was showing off—*no hands!*—on the monkey bars and fell, breaking both wrists. That evening, his two arms were shrouded in blinding white plaster casts. We all sat down to dinner, Jim at the head of our table opposite Dad, at the other head. My parents, who could bury the needle of scales that measured the expression of agitation, were impressively calm through their kids' many visits to the emergency ward for stitches and broken bones.

As the only leftie I took my designated place next to Jim on a bench where my arm would not bump anyone. I recall how cool Jim looked with his badges of honor, two shining casts and some dried scabs on his head as we ate dinner.

That evening, my new precocious older friend, Susan B., stared at Jim as he came out our cellar door with his band—he must've sung as they played. She told me that Jim was "cute," a word I had not ever heard applied to older boys, only babies. Susan explained, that Jim looked like movie stars—Tommy Sands, Fabian, and Ricky Nelson. I began to see my brother in a new light—his thick straight black hair (combed pompadour style of course), black eyes, swarthy skin were what made a boy cute. Oh, all my brothers were cute then.

Even Jim would agree that he was Dad's anointed one, which was far from an unmixed blessing. This meant that Jim got the best (heartfelt encouragement) and the worst (too many whacks, too much criticism, too many judgments) of Dad's parenting skills and the net benefit is something only Jim can assess. Dad was a tough disciplinarian and any modern psychologist would agree, his toughness, bordering on physical abuse by today's standards, was a projection outward of the self-criticism he never came to terms with.

Jim bears Dad's father's name, typical of Sicilian families. (Chuck is named for Dad). It is no small wonder that all of my brothers are classic over-achievers, driven Type As. Fortunately, where Dad was excessive with alcohol and moodiness, they are so with work and accomplishments. My father was boastful of his kids but he was too tough on all of us, using his hands, belt, and severe restrictions, but especially with his boys, whom he forbade upon pain of death to "disgrace my name." He would banish the boys to the cellar without supper for some minor infraction, like being a little late. One whole summer Grace and I were restricted to our backyard for not being in sight when our parents were ready to leave for a visit to Grandma's.

One school night I was up in my bedroom studying when the whole house shook as if huge boulders were being tossed upon it. Everyone ran downstairs to find Dad having one of his seismic explosions, pouncing on a brother. I cannot recall the details of this wild display but I can recall with some chagrin that its effect on me was perversely voyeuristic. I was privy to pending disaster, happening to *someone else not me*. To recast Tolstoy's famous pronouncement, all families generate stress. My family absorbed and channeled our unique brand—Dad's post-traumatic stress.

Among the threads that bind my siblings are, not only our shared surviving Dad and his PTS, and explosions, but that our filial love of Dad also survives. When Charlie was good, he was stupendously wonderful, creative, charming, sensitive, humorous, humble, expansive, encouraging, insightful, life affirming, even mystical. He has lived long enough for us to see and pity his own fragility, to get a perspective on his flaws, to see life cut him down to size, as it will for all of us, and to have him say he was sorry for being so hard on us, for his being so flawed.

This summer day we are hard on ourselves. Jim, Chuck, and I plan to summit Mount Whitney from the steeper east side, in one day. I pick Jim up in Palo Alto and we make the eight-hour drive in my dumpy un-air-conditioned car. We chat about his wife, Jane, who is so far surviving her breast cancer, and planning to renovate their home—she is a skilled carpenter, classical pianist, and accomplished artist. I do a little ranting against mammograms. Jane had just had a negative one when she found the stage four lump herself.

We talk about my Zen Buddhist practice, in which I have recently received lay ordination, about our siblings. Recently my brother Tom told me that he had gone with Jim and Chuck to see the Vietnam Memorial on the Mall in Washington D.C. We had all been to our sister Lisa's wedding in the area. Chuck found the name of one of his buddies on the huge black granite block that commemorates that war's more than 58,000 missing and dead. In a rare display, he was overwhelmed with emotion and Jim hugged him. I wished I had been there but it was good to hear about my brothers bonding, something my sisters and I do more naturally.

I tell Jim about all my comical bear encounters in the Sierra with Chuck. And the one with my boyfriend Dan and his sister Julie. Dan, Julie, and I had just turned in for the night to our tent in Sequoia National Park when we heard the pacing of a four-legged creature. It was a big black bear, his perplexed golden eyes boring through us. The soft depression and berry-laden scat should've been a dead giveaway that we were in some bear's sleeping spot. We broke camp lickety-split in the dark and scampered up Black Mountain yelling to the bear *Sorry, bear, sorry.*

"It was funny," I say, "I felt like when I used to run away from my brothers, screaming bloody murder, *I'm telling Dad!*"

Inevitably we talk about Dad, who is ever on the brink of catastrophic heart problems. How many times have we thought this is the end and rallied around him only to have him bounce back, jump in the Lincoln Continental with Mom, and drive to his annual Army buddy reunion somewhere across the country (those reunions must be like hair of the dog—war—that bit him). Modern medicine has kept Dad ticking beyond the years he should have died, given the abuse he heaped on his body. We know Dad can't have many years left and we all have this sense of his dying being like a huge rock rolled away. Dad casts a long shadow and we wonder if we'll be ready to face the sunshine when he is gone.

I brag to Jim about my partner, Dan, whom I've been living with now for several years. How his Murphy side of the family came successfully over the same Sierra Nevada pass the year before the infamous Donner Party and has been tagged California's First Irish Family. How the Sierra Foothill town of Murphys is named for Dan's great (several greats) uncles, John and Dan Murphy, the first to strike it rich during the California Gold Rush, only to squander the family fortune by the time Dan's parents came along. How the town of Yuba is named for Dan's great, great (maybe another great, not sure, does it matter?) aunt, Elizabeth Yuba-Murphy. How Dan's maternal Grandmother Kelly was a schoolteacher in Bodie, now a preserved ghost town in Nevada. I envy Dan his deep-time connection to California my adopted home.

I think about waxing rhapsodic to Jim about how vital this deep connection to land is to our whole being (and may be missing for us); how we all need to have a homegrown dreamspot, a sort of sacred retreat, a place where the sights, sounds, smells are so familiar year after year they lend a feeling of mind-body joy. We cultivate that dreamspot by staying put in place. I came to this little epiphany after reading *Good, Wild, and Sacred*, an essay in *Co-Evolutionary Quarterly* by Pulitzer-prize-winning poet Gary Snyder.

I keep this to myself, as it contradicts the way we've moved around a lot, have not stayed put. The restless spell that keeps us all moving comes down through our parents. We ride in silence the last languid hour down the east side of the Sierra. Desert heat and the view of the mountains—a multi-horned sleeping rhinoceros always comes to my mind—forestall speech. Maybe I am cultivating a dreamspot in the Sierra by returning year after year crosses my hazy mind.

We find Chuck inside the visitor center at Lone Pine talking to a ranger. Chuck informs us that we cannot get a permit to hike up Whitney. The daily quota has been reached. Then he says to the ranger, "I could do the technical route but these two . . . I doubt it." Jim and I chuckle with Chuck the comedian. We can get a permit to climb Whitney's (14,505 feet) neighboring peak, Mount Langley (14,042 feet). What's 463 feet lower? Chump change.

I've already summited, or *bagged*, Whitney, as the fourteeners say. There are a bunch of peaks over 14,000 feet in California. Some require technical skills to bag. The time I summited Whitney with the three Charlies we reached it from the west side of the Sierra, taking a weeklong backpack trip to reach it. The west is called the gentler side, but still, we had actually started on the east side and crisscrossed the snowy range, trudging over three mountain passes over 12,000 feet.

The boys and I are not too disappointed. Thousands of hikers set out to climb Whitney from the east side and I recall the day we came down that way in 1995. The number of people attempting the climb in a day was only less startling than the quality of some. They were visibly old and not in shape, looking haggard before they even reached a quarter of the way up from base camp. I also recall my vertigo on the way down. There were patches of old snow and ice where iron railings had been installed so you didn't slip to your certain death.

I identify easily with Mount Langley, Whitney's kid sister ever in the latter's shadow. Langley, the farthest south of California's fourteeners, has much to recommend it, not least of all its less human traffic. According to the technical climbers who are able to scale its craggy face, the view from Langley's summit includes Whitney, the Owen's Valley, and the Great Western Divide.

We drive up Whitney Portal road to the parking area, then have to hike about six miles with close to 2,000-feet elevation gain to our base camp, Cottonwood Lakes. Chuck sets up a two-person tent for Jim and him and I set up my trusty old Kelty tent. Not having seen a cloud in the sky and not wanting to carry the weight, I have left my tent's rain cover behind. I should know better by now that quixotic Sierra weather can change on a smile or frown. But so far, so good. I'm taking a calculated risk, I think.

I look around at the trembling cottonwoods and the calm lakes and think I could return here over and over and dream my life away. I would make my dark roast coffee in the morning, write until afternoon, bathe in the lakes, build a fire to cook dinner. Ahh, the simple primitive that I am at times forgets all about the city life and the things I love there. But never mind.

"Where's your fly?" asks Chuck in a parental tone when he sees my naked tent set up.

"It won't rain," I say. "Hey, look at that clark's nutcracker that just flew overhead."

"You ain't coming in my tent," says Chuck. Famous last words.

"No rain is in the forecast," I say. *A fine thing to be independent of clothing where it is so hard to carry,* I quote John Muir under my breath, from *My First Summer in the Sierra.*

We boil water, pour it over dried food—Mountain High's chicken in pine needle cream sauce or something good—that taste stunningly delicious to me. We turn in early under a sky so perforated with stars and smeared with the cream of Milky Way it makes the heart ache and wonder where the dark matter really lives. I fall asleep reading a fable from my palm-sized *Zen Flesh, Zen Bones.* The fifth admonition on Centering reads *Consider your essence as light rays rising from center to center up the vertebrae, and so rises livingness in you.* Perfect tune for the star beams.

We sleep well, no rain, and are up before dawn, have coffee and a quick breakfast, are packed and ready with Jim and me only slightly behind *el Lider Born-To-Run Carlos.* We have some twenty-one miles round-trip to summit Langley and want to make it back to camp before nightfall.

The route is splendid. What I can describe about the beauty and magnificence of Sierra high country is said better by others—two California authors in particular and one from New Jersey come to mind. John Muir, of course, strode the Sierra's bowls, basins, cirques, glaciers, toothy summits and their crannies; communed with its foxtail, Jeffrey, and white pines; hung out in a lodgepole; contemplated the teal blue of lakes, snowmelt of cascades and streams; and devoured the craggy views from every angle. He then sat down with pen and turned the minutest of this sensory detail into lyrical narrative and luminous prose that today makes a nature lover salivate.

"How sweet and keen the air! Every breath a blessing," wrote the Scottish immigrant of the high mountains in *My First Summer in the Sierra.* "Here the sugar pine reaches its fullest development in size and beauty and number of individuals, filling every swell and hollow and down-plunging ravine almost to the exclusion of other species. A few yellow pines are still to be found as companions, and in the coolest places silver firs; but noble as these are, the sugar pine is king, and spreads long protecting arms above them while they rock and wave in sign of recognition."

It is Sacramento native Joan Didion I think of as we hike past calm meadow ponds, tiers of lakes, and streams, who in her artfully condensed prose gave me the vision of the Sierra as a "granite keep." I love the surreal image of crystalline water falling, falling from these mountains into our open mouths at sea level. Once on a trip out of White Wolf with Chuck, I swam in the Tuolumne River marveling at the fluid that journeys by way of Hetch Hetchy to the classical Pulgas Water Temple there to flow through my kitchen faucet. New Jerseyan John McPhee, who admitted that the geological terms, like orogeny, can "stir the groin," summed up the broadest view of this range that tickles my soles, soul, and muse equally. He described the Sierra en masse, which is really the crust of planet earth cantilevered upward through the pelvic thrusting of tectonic plates, as a giant blimp, or literally an erection. *Granite,* I learned from McPhee, is a blanket description for many variations of that igneous composition, or earthy sexual emission, since I'm stooping to that metaphor.

I breathe deeply the fragrant piney air and maybe it's just the coffee working my adrenals, or maybe it's the joy of hiking with the boys—at last—but I have a burst of ecstasy. It is a feeling so sublime that requires no explanation. If I ignore my modern clothes and gear, this could be any century of recent eras. External stimulation is pared down to rock, wood, water, soil, that which has thrived here perhaps as long as time mathematics. And here I am so in my body, my mind sweetly flatlined as I put one foot in front of the other. Ecstasy, I have learned, is like our breath—you can't hold it, you must let it go. The moment passes. I still feel high.

My brothers are both in front of me, out of earshot. I'm the tortoise, gleeful at my own pace that allows me the solitude to turn in or out at whim. Amid a silent stretch I hear the buzz of an insect. In my timeless reverie I confuse it with a frequent summer sound in New Jersey, the saw-like buzzing of my brother Salvatore's remote-controlled toy, a red, decal-laden hot rod I had watched

Sal assemble. I think about the summer songs—by the Beach Boys and Sonny & Cher—that I loved on AM radio and that filled my long days when I never left the block we lived on, how summers were the best times of our childhoods. I think my brothers would agree. No matter how far we've traveled, the Jersey Shore that summer gave us for less than a week's time each year is unmatched.

The jaunts down the shore to Mom's brother, Uncle Pat's home in Lavalette dominate my happy memory bank. Mom and Dad wedged us in the station wagon along with crates of summer produce and food. The adults laughed a lot, drank icy cocktails. The kids lived in bathing suits at the beach and if we were lucky got a buck to go on the wild mouse and play ski ball or a spinning wheel game at Seaside Heights.

Almost seems sacrilegious to let my mind wander back to New Jersey here in this sacred ground of nature. But I have long mused over how the seasons, so unmarked and jumbled in my mind in San Francisco, are what help me gauge the time and place of stored memories. *Personal truths emerge from the wilderness,* I read somewhere.

I retrieve that Gary Snyder essay, *Good, Wild, and Sacred*, that inspired a significant sea change in the way I think of place and connect to it. *We have no one to teach us which parts of the landscape were once thought to be sacred* has been a repeating mantra for years now.

I do not begrudge my accident of birth in a place where *wilderness* referred to anything but this untrammeled, pristine, natural earthy habitat. I come to the Sierra as who I am. My inner power and dreams were bred in cities, in a crowded household, with a domineering father, submissive mother. I am no less capable than Snyder of mind-body joy. Thanks to him, I have the sense of finding what was never lost.

Like my two big brothers walking this path in front of me, I got my kicks in a thriving industrial metropolis in the most densely populated state, at one time extremely polluted. We grew up under patriarchal rule in the strictest sense—nature, and women by extension, is under man's dominion. When our peers in the country were qualifying for scout badges or attending 4-H events, my closest sister, Grace, and I were partying among the bad-ass boys, driving over to Staten Island to drink or bussing over to Greenwich Village to blend in with hippies. Now look at us. Serenity's finest hour comes in getting far from pavement, far from a flush toilet.

Snyder has tended to his mountain farmstead in the Sierra Nevada foothills since the 1960s. In his essay he talks of the benefits of our becoming a "place-centered" culture again. We are a continuation of our habitat. He calls it being a "cosmopolitan local." That makes me feel OK with loving the city as much as the mountains, needing the culture of one, the retreat to the other.

Reading Snyder's essay gave me pause. I did some reckoning and counted twenty-three address changes over nineteen years. They included two countries (the U.S. and France) and four states (New Jersey, California, Pennsylvania, and Utah).

I had not set out to be so promiscuous in my relationship to place. I realized I had lost something—the constancy of place, of intimacy with the same dirt, rain, and air year after year—that I had, having lived my childhood in the same home with the same people. A grief was welling up in me.

Society puts out-sized focus on the institution of marriage and its speculative relation to crumbling ethics. But becoming unconnected to our land, to place, is much more directly linked to large scale planetary problems— environmental, social, political, health, and maybe all psychological disorders.

When we were hunters and gatherers, writes Snyder, all places were considered good, wild, *and* sacred. Wild nature was not perceived as disordered and we "drew on the spread of richness." We became an agrarian-based race and began to separate *good* land from *wild* land. Good came to refer to land that we can figuratively and literally harness and cultivate, "land that is productive of very specific plants." Today, "wild means unmanipulated, unmanaged natural habitat," but not necessarily good. Before we separated good from wild, all land was sacred. Eventually sacred came to refer to "ritually cultivated land or special temple fields." We started to treat land and each other differently.

"In the industrialized world," says Snyder, "it's not that nothing is sacred; it's that sacred is sacred and that's all that is sacred." Such compartmentalization is not healthy. Some land is "saved like a virgin priestess, some is overworked endlessly like a wife; some is brutally publicly reshaped, like an exuberant girl declared promiscuous and punished. Good, wild, and sacred couldn't be farther apart."

I mentally reunite the virgin, the wife, and the girl and lead the holy alliance back to the mountains where the sun is strong and warm and glistens on patches of old snow. There is hope, says Snyder, for our dis-*placed* race. We need to listen, he advises, like the most musical of creatures that we are. "The nature spirits are never dead, they are alive under our feet, over our heads, all around us, ready to speak when we are silent and centered."

While I have been gathering the wool of such thoughts, Chuck, has been orienteering. He tells us about how we must be sure to take the Old Army Pass, not the New Army Pass, which would have us lose elevation then need to regain it. We actually get it right and hours later are all dragging as we crunch over the last plateau of talus and scree. Chuck's fingers are bluish—cyanosis, it's called. My rock 'n' roll brother Jim has never seemed so zombie-like. Just before the summit, we help each other to climb a very steep chute of menacing boulders, scrambling on all fours.

234

I recall the summit of Whitney was as busy as an open-air shopping mall. Langley's summit is less frenzied and I don't mind its nondescript rock and sand. We rest but not for long as the climb to sudden altitude is dimming our faculties. Oh yes, we are dimwits: There at the top, we learn that there was a gentler, less precipitous ascent than that rocky chute. We laugh at our inefficiency. We are newcomers still warming up to these cold mountains.

We take the easy way down. Chuck's fingers regain color, Jim comes back from zombiedom, and I whimsically make a mental notch in my imaginary belt— bagged my second fourteener. The scenery never looks the same to me on the return trip, perhaps due to shifting light and perspective, not to mention lower blood sugar, and I just hope that *el Líder* brother of mine is not leading us astray.

We make it home to Cottonwood Lakes well before dark and although we are beyond spent, we all have that second glorious wind, that psyche rush that comes with accomplishment (Dad's dark validating eyes saying *I expect nothing less of you kids*). Jim and Chuck stand around, talking shop, maybe about business, maybe about Jim's business Catalytica Associates that recently went public and, and, well, don't ask me to chat you up on stock market stuff. I plead "e-numerate," the numbers version of illiterate.

Even our base camp, close to or above 10,000 feet, is pretty high, but we are acclimating to the rarefied air. When we were kids the boys took paths girls couldn't, mysterious paths, secret trails. Now we have walked the same one to thin air heights. In camp there are no girl-boy tasks, just chores to be done to eat, stay dry, warm. Did I say dry?

We climb inside our tents with our weary bones. It's been such a gratifying day. First we see the lightning, then feel and hear the rumble of thunder. *Consider your essence as light rays* . . . I meditate as the light torches the mountain, less and less distant.

"Um, Chuck? Jim?" I say softly. Silence. "You guys awake? It's raining." I hear a pretend snore. Then, "Come on over."

I crowd into a two-person tent with Chuck and Jim. We position our sleeping bags head to foot, like sardines. If one moves, we all have to move. It really feels like old times back on Price Street. We issue a group decree of no snoring. We are quiet, then Chuck begins singing, "We are the Cusumanos." I think of saying, "Like John Muir said, 'Going to the mountains is going home.' " But soon, despite the crush, we are all falling out fast into deep dreamless sleep.

18

Blue-belly Lizards, Rattlesnakes, and Evangelist, 2002

I'm deep in alpha brain waves, following the rhythm of stepping with my poles like a four-legged creature, as we backpack through the Tuolumne Canyon. I am chewing on details of a friend's recent death, feeling angry about her dying. She was ninety, a surrogate mother—wild, liberal, Cal Berkeley educated, a card-carrying Commie who took refuge in Villa del Bravo along with Dalton Trumbo, Ring Larder, and other witch-hunted and black-listed luminaries in the '50s. We met when she had settled into being a student of Zen Buddhism.

To validate my anger, the pile of brown leaves off to my left begins to swirl upward, out of perfect stillness. A worried eddy of air out of nowhere rises above the ground several inches. It's cartoonish. I snap back to the present and see this picture with a shock. I am staring at a squiggling diamond-patterned back of an agitated rattlesnake.

In the short space of time during which I freeze, I have many thoughts. Maybe we are delirious. This year is going on eight years of our backpack compulsion. It truly is a passion, an obsession, and a just a tiny bit of a compulsion.

But never mind that. So much of life, from the nine-to-five workday to the acquisitive "consumptive" behavior—is some mix of those three. And we just had to do this trip that promises some new and beautiful scenery through the Pate Valley of the Yosemite area, views of the Hetch Hetchy Reservoir, and a walk through the Tuolumne Canyon with a chance to bathe in the water I drink and that is three-quarters of my body's composition. It will be forty-six grueling miles.

Before I decide what to do about the snake—we were warned about them and about the non-venomous blue-bellied lizards—I want to finish my thoughts of Anne. I was her scribe and each week would put her hand-written memoirs online. What a life she had, from privileged Pacific Heights to social activist to Buddhist. I did not want to replace my own mother, whose eightieth birthday was yesterday, only add Anne to my pantheon of influential elders. Anne seemed so alive. But the doctors told her that her heart was weak. So there she went, as if to prove them right, off into the wild beyond. I blame the doctors, not her mortality.

Dear Mr. Rattler, can't we say die? Uncle? Give up the ghost of our born-to-move bodies and just go to the seashore like normal people and slather on sunscreen instead of insect repellent? Couldn't we have llamas, mules, or horses pack our gear into the backcountry for us?

This snake does not commune with humans. It would not rear its head on the High Sierra camps, which I've just done with Dan and his sister Julie, who are conspicuously absent from our trips of late (there is talk of the "Chuck Factor," meaning moving at a rip-roaring pace). Chuck would never entertain the idea of that *soft* approach to the wilderness. There is a lottery to get on the popular camps and twice now Julie has gotten places for us. You carry only a light daypack. The camps are sturdy canvas-covered lodges with beds and dining rooms—no need to hang food from bears. Your gear is transported for you each day. You are fed gourmet breakfasts and luscious dinners and given bag lunches. The six lodges include Tuolumne, Sunrise, Merced Lake, Vogelsang, May Lakes, and Glen Aulin. So Civilized. John Muir would approve. But not Chuck.

Back to the rattler. I guess I had better do something. I love the way the snake moves seemingly in place, like the valleys and troughs of the letter W. I suppose I must have put my walking stick right down on the poor shade-seeking reptile. It did not appreciate that disturbance. My adrenaline is laid back on this hot, dry, dusty trail. But by and by it kicks in as my fascination with rattlers, who look like a large piece of exotic jewelry, turns to bragging rights. I run to tell Chuck who is always about a half mile in front of me.

Five feet long! (OK, it was really about three feet long.)

What does Chuck do? Not to be outdone, later this day he encounters a rattler, who hisses at Chuck's pole. Chuck tries to snap its picture. It is not a beauty shot. We are delirious on this trip, barely able to keep atop of our bodies' need for hydration.

Can't we say die? Just this once? Llamas, mules, horses, next time. I promise myself.

We left from White Wolf Lodge yesterday morning in a rush, on the trail out of our minds, by 9:30 a.m. We dutifully phoned Mom for her eightieth birthday, for which we'll all meet in New Jersey later this summer and celebrate. When my turn to toast her comes up, I will tell about the dream I had years ago and have never forgotten. *I'm trying to cook a chicken in the oven. But I need Mom's help. She blithely leans over the oven and has to open ten doors. I marvel that she can do this and stick her arm in the oven without getting burned.* I leave the obvious analysis to the reader. What I like about the dream is that it allows me to find some mystical depth to my mother whose life I have never emulated.

White Wolf Lodge is just outside the Yosemite boundary and it should have been a fortifying start for us. But we had way too much downhill our first day, for a tally of 10.5 hot, dry miles. The uphill is preferable as it's easier on the toes and the knees. I loved the view to Hetch Hetchy, that paramecium-shape of navy blue, the dam built on the Tuolumne that we in San Francisco may drink, the O'Shaughnessy dam that broke John Muir's heart when that valley was flooded. I could have sat on the granite ledge where there was a precious breeze, rare on this trip, forever.

I loved the incense cedars in the Pate Valley. We met a guy on the way here who reminded me of Tom Hanks, not Chuck though. He told us Pate Valley was "nothing— trailer camp trash there." I disagreed completely. I loved the quiet valley feel. On the way down when I saw my first meadow I got that sweet, grassy meadow nostalgia. I don't know what it is about meadows but they are at once calming and arousing.

This second day out is no easier. We are almost to the Water Wheel Falls. I see a beautiful tiger lily and some groundsel on our way to distract me.

I write in my journal, *It's been a brutal trip. We got off on the wrong foot. The trip's been very hot, even at night. Too much down, down, down. It hurts my calves, quads, hips so badly I was doing a backwards crawl.*

We were brought up never allowed to say *I'm tired* or *I can't.* That inner parent is tyrannizing us, keeping us pushing beyond our comfort, through pain and weakness. We are now trudging through what the guidebook calls "the inner sanctum" of the Tuolumne Canyon and for at least two hours now I want to drop my backpack and take a dip. But Chuck keeps saying, we have to cover more miles. We keep passing luscious green pools of water that beg me to dip into them. I am so ragged inside.

It is evening now. I am trying to decide if Chuck is dead or just not moving in his sleep. He retreated to his tent without dinner, something I would never do. I took a dip in the river and washed my clothes, ate some Kung pao chicken alone. We had to stake camp at this not so nice site, the last one. It is messy with forest debris and has a lot of yellow jackets. When we arrived, I heard an uncharacteristic groan of sorrow come from Chuck. He was looking at a dead bird lying under a big fallen log, the bird on its back, its claws upward in rigor mortis. It looked like a jay drained of its blue color.

"You think some animal killed it and is coming back for it?" Chuck asked.

"Well, not a bear, they don't eat birds, maybe a coyote or mountain lion."

We had to move it away from our site, so I pushed away my fear of symbolism and prodded the avian corpse with my pole, light as its feathers, to the rocky bank of the Tuolumne. Awake for hours now, I'm gathering dark wool. The bird was an omen. Chuck is not moving because he died quietly. His last words were "I don't feel good." (That's not what I'll tell Cheri, though.) His heart must have just stopped. It has beat its allotted lub dubs. For hours he has not made a sound and usually he snores somewhat throughout his sleep cycle. I don't feel like getting up from my sleeping bag and checking his pulse. In case he's just out cold. It's so hot. I'll tell Cheri how excited he was for their upcoming anniversary. Before, like the blue jay, he joined the Great Spirit in the Sky. By the time he makes a sound I am exhausted.

The next day Chuck agrees to say die. We can short circuit the loop by going out of the backcountry by way of Glen Aulin, the High Sierra Camp. There we pitch our tents and eat in the dining hall. There is a cascade nearby with the healing negative ions of moving water.

Just the thought of bailing affords comfort and energy. As we hike toward our refuge, I fall into my standard contemplation, thinking how Catholicism is dualistic, positing God or god outside of us. And odd synchronicity occurs in the shape of an unsettling encounter with a Christian evangelist. Here, of all places, in the gods' country. He looks harmless enough upon first sight, dressed in clean khaki, slightly balding, groomed beard, fiftyish—certainly less threatening than a pit viper. He eagerly tells me upon little prompting that he is a Christian minister who preaches abstinence in Uganda and Kenya to deal with the AIDS epidemic. "But," he adds even before I counter attack, "the international orgs are coming in and ruining it by teaching safe sex.

I gather myself up and say, "Abstinence is fine but if you can't what's wrong with safe sex?"

"It doesn't work. We found it has a 15 percent failure rate. Only abstinence works."

I should have said, 15 percent, not bad. Instead I said, walking into his waiting trap, "If you can't abstain . . . it's human nature . . ."

His canned response is all ready, "As Katharine Hepburn said in the *African Queen*, 'We were put on this earth to rise above human nature.' "

Kate Hepburn, of all people to call on to support his nonsense! But before I can get into a heated discussion with the creep, Chuck who is resting on a granite bench pipes up and interrupts in a loud voice, "*African Queen* was a great movie! And I'm not getting into any more of this argument." I stand up from my granite seat and in a huff grab my poles and say, "Yeah, great movie."

243

I want to stay and clean up that fundamentalist's wrong thinking but I have to keep up with Chuck. Humph, I thought only pagans and pantheists backpacked in the Sierra, I grouse to Chuck who has no interest in sharing my concern that the evil-angelist is actually spreading AIDS.

Now, if only I had my sisters with me. They'd not be indifferent. We could rehabilitate this misinformed man about abstinence and safe sex in five easy pieces. Tina could talk non-sense into him about how abstinence works, yeah right. Donna would mime safe sex methods similar to a flight attendant showing how to unbuckle belts, put on oxygen mask. Grace, a registered nurse, would take the man's vitals as he listened, as I was holding his arms gently, and Lisa was wiping his tears. Terry would offer a free post-rehab therapy session. We'd fix his thinking but good.

Instead of sharing my indignation, Chuck distracts me by pointing to a granite explosion frozen on the horizon. "Look a cowboy on his horse that has bent its head to drink." It works. I think of my boyfriend, Dan, back home, who wisely opted out of this trip, who has deep *terroir*, connection to the Sierra, who would approve of Chuck's wild imaginative interpretation.

Glen Aulin is the Ritz as far as we are concerned. We get hot showers and a dinner of butter-tender filet mignon which we can eat sitting on chairs at a real table. There is no chance of reptiles at this elevation but a rogue bear cub tramps through camp in broad daylight looking for a handout or unattended stash. He'll have to be relocated if he keeps it up.

We spend two nights at Glen Aulin with few incidents, nothing to debate, just thinking about the family reunion for Mom at the Jersey Shore—yay, sun, sand, sea, and pizza pie. We hardly give a nod to the fact that we actually rose above our human nature, that in all of our backpacking history this is a first, cutting off miles so save ourselves. The backpacker's equivalent of safe sex.

19

Follow Your Wildest Dreams, 2004

"Dad! Dad!" I shout. He keeps floating by taller than life, like Casper the Friendly Ghost coming out a swirling lower body. His expression is solemn and he barely acknowledges me as if he can't because he is a spirit. I run into someone at work (VIA Magazine) but she cannot see him, yet he appears every time I say Dad! I run into Cheri and say Dad! This time he floats by, shaking his head No. What does he mean?

Chuck and I are old hands now at our backpack trips going on more than ten years. We have the food and equipment down to a science, and each other's quirks and our repartee. This year we are doing a splendid trip out of Mineral King in Sequoia Kings Canyon. To get to the trailhead we have to drive twenty-five miles up a steep winding road—takes more than an hour. It's lovely. Mineral King is where Sierra Club fought off Goliath, a ski resort developer, in the sixties. The would-be developer was Walt Disney.

I have the above dream our first night out and since dreams have always been taken seriously by my parents, their portent discussed at length, I contemplate what my father is trying to tell me. My father has only been dead for two months. This seems rather premature for him to start showing up in my dreams. He died in bed next to my mother with six of us kids sprawled around their home on

June 22, Father's Day and the Summer Solstice. Grace, Terry, and I had been trying to "midwife" passage of his soul into the next sphere. We kept him calm and Terry sang *Danny Boy*, because Dad loved that song about a soldier. A soprano sang it at his wake. At the end of his life, he became more and more possessed by his war record and wanted to get the Purple Heart he had been too proud to seek back in 1945. It was too late, but he did get the Bronze Star, thanks to New Jersey Senator Torricelli.

My mother woke up at 3 AM and knew he was gone. After the coroner took away the body I had one of those creepy intimations—that he was not really dead. A sort of denial or a form of buyer's remorse (I did want him to go peacefully)? Even when a parent's death is age-appropriate (Dad was 84), unknown ramifications loom when he or she dies. Dad was the major protagonist in our family narrative. Would our plot go soft and flaccid or would we discover sub-plots lurking and find new meaning? Dreaming about a dead person usually meant a birth, but there are none in the family oven that I know of. A psychological death and re-birth is the farthest thing from my mind at this moment.

I have already done this backpack trip out of Mineral King with Dan and his sister Julie—the trip was marked by the famous bear whose lair we camped in until he shushed us away, into the black of night. I think how Dan always intimated that the wilderness trips, which mainly came in the summer, were when he felt closest to me. Hmmmm, I always thought, if only we could be swept away in time and space to the magical spot in the backcountry . . .

This trip is remarkably smooth considering Chuck's and my history. I like to think we've been immunized by recent snafus during spring desert trips. In the New York Mountains of the Mojave National Preserve, the fierce wind bent Chuck's $300-tent pole and buffeted our own bones badly. On a trip to Anza-Borrego Desert State Park, we backpacked in several miles down a sandy wash to what we thought was a remote peaceful area, only to learn that the wash was a road we could have driven. We watched other four-wheel vehicles drive by. Bob Hope & Bing Crosby on the road to meet Stan Laurel & Oliver Hardy.

The Mineral King loop will cover nearly fifty miles through some of the most beautiful parts of the Sierra. The first day out we climb steeply up a flank of lush meadow blazing with the gold of Bigelow's sneezeweed and cobalt blue of gentian. What a breathtaking splash the wild flowers make this year.

Dawdling in the duff, motating up a mountain (Black Rock) that is so naked and vertigo inducing, I find this trip has all the beauteous high points of my favorite Sierra backcountry: purple sky, silver granite, the red bark of a foxtail forest, the green waters of Nine Lakes Basin. Every site custom-fits our day's end survival needs—Pinto Lake,

Little Five Lakes, Big Arroyo—and the Redwood Grove Meadow, oh my, is a fairy tale. Two men sit inside the hollowed trunk of a sequoia tree, making peanut butter sandwiches. The gods are good to all this year.

But what about the dream?

At Cliff Creek, the rushing water sings me to sleep with a Tom Jones song, *It's Not Unusual*. From Cliff Creek to Timber Gap, I think about how the hard work of backpacking is what Diane Ackerman calls "deep play."

Still, a mantra, *next year llamas*, repeats throughout the trip.

At Cliff Creek, we meet Bill, who has come all the way from Indiana, to deep play in America's purple mountain majesty. He asks us to call his wife on Sunday when we get out. Later, I joke, "Everyone he meets he asks to call his wife." Chuck mimics her, *Yeah, whatta you want, you're the hundredth person to call me!* We have a good laugh and of course call her and report our healthy Bill sighting—to her relief.

In camp, the night before we have to hike to Bearpaw Meadow, eponymous with its denizens, I compose a song:

If You're Going to Bearpaw Meadow
(To tune of *If You're Going to San Francisco*)

If you're going to Bearpaw Meadow
You will see food strung up in the air
For the bears at Bearpaw Meadow

Know lots of ways
To get inside your gear

All across the Meadow
It's a bit unsettled
Campers in motion
Big bears with notions

If you're going to Bearpaw Meadow
Better know how to hang food in the air
Or the bears in Bearpaw Meadow
Will leave claw marks
And get inside your gear.

My dream. I finally decide it is Dad telling me to *follow my dream*s. I'm a bit perplexed because I have always done so, not having the burden of producing grandchildren for him. I wanted to be a writer and although it didn't bring me fortune or fame, that is exactly what I managed to do my whole professional life. But something gnaws at me now. I could hardly imagine that in a little more than a year's time all will be revealed. The saying goes that if you want to make the gods laugh tell them *your* plans. But what tricksters those immortals be.

Let me back up a bit. In 2002, when I return from Cuba, I have an irresistible yen to learn salsa. An image in Cuba struck my eye like a divine spark. A chocolate-skinned woman whose body moves like warm taffy dances salsa, her legs gleaming out of slits in her frilly bellbottoms. I have to learn that dance.

I start with Arthur Murray back home in San Francisco but quickly get their number. They want to hold me back so I can keep doling out the dough. Across town at the Metronome, I find a wealth of teachers who nurture my dancing. I get proficient in salsa as well as swing— West Coast and Lindy—and some ballroom dances that I love, foxtrot and waltz. It's all soulful recreation. Another of Dad's aphorisms: *You can't not smile when you dance.* Fellow dancers insist I try Argentine tango, but I tell them it has no allure for me. The gods believe otherwise.

OK, I'll try it. Daniel and Pier teach me the eight-count basic, Eldon Bryce, Andrea Fuchilieri, and Christy Cote each teach me the embrace and connection, the walk, how to do figure eights, windmill turns, fancy leg kicks called *boleos*. Before I know it or *plan* on it, I am hooked on Argentine tango and that is all I am dancing. The gods no longer laugh, the smug beings. They have their way.

Quit my job, leave my boyfriend, move to Buenos Aires? For a dance?

No way, I tell them.

Way, they say.

Long ago, I read *Save Me the Waltz* by Zelda Fitzgerald. My girlfriend who lent me the book told me *They put Zelda away because she wouldn't stop trying to be a tap dancer.*

So? I asked. What was wrong with that?

251

She was too old—twenty-seven.

Double that number in my case.

Quit my job, leave my boyfriend of many years, move to Buenos Aires? For a dance?

That is a precise summary of what the sequence of events will be a year and a half after this Mineral King trip.

How was I to know the gods would speak to me through the hundreds of men's torsos I would lean into in tango? A primal form of braille? The language of tango, I can only say, predates that of human speech. It is experiential and if I start riffing on why, how, what it is about tango, I will only defile the experience that only grows deeper, stronger, more and more divine. And yet so human.

Llamas. Mules. Horses. Any beast of burden, be on call. The writing has been on the tree trunk for two years now. After we cut our Tuolumne Canyon trip short, the following year, another bail: Red's Meadow to Mono Pass, we never made Mono Pass. My boyfriend Dan was with us this time and in an all-for-one, one-for-all decision we scuttled at Thomas Edison Lake, taking the coolest backcountry ferry across the lake. We paid a price, $300 taxi, to drive east over the Sierra back to our cars.

So, it turns out this will be one of my last *pure* backpack trips. Not that I will stop going into the wilderness questing for whatever it is the gods deem me worthy. I still need that renewal. I need to have my doors of perception cleansed by sleeping on dirt. These trips are my "spas" of life. There will be room in my closet for hiking boots and more than a dozen pairs of spike heels. Who knew?

Soon after the Mineral King trip, I will decide I must preserve my feet, ankles, knees, and all my joints for tango, which I will eventually teach, a tango missionary (Hey, remember that abstinence evangelizer? I will go to Kenya and teach slum-dwelling kids tango, a dancing form of safe sex. Put that in your thumping bible, Mister Sperminator.) I will miss a few years in the Sierra, living down south of the equator, but will eventually return home and join Sierra Club mule pack trips. The mules carry the weight. We hike in unburdened to a base camp. So civilized. My brother Chuck only gets faster without me in tow. When possible, I camp and meet him at the exit trail from his backcountry trip. He goes on to do the Whitney hike we had done in 1995 in two nights instead of the week it took us when much younger. Dad must've told Chuck to follow his dreams too. Donna, the baby, has a major transformation. After years of putting her degrees to good use as a cocktail waitress, she straightens up and flies right into the arms of a plum United Nations job. Jim, the oldest, will go on to new never-dreamed-possible lives. After working his tush off as a research scientist, then as an executive in corporate America and co-founder and CEO of two public Silicon Valley technology companies, Jim will, incredibly, become the executive producer of an internationally-distributed feature film (*What Matters Most*), then proceed to serve as owner of an award-winning five-star Holistic Castle Hotel and Spa in the Czech Republic. Oh, and in his spare time he will write books on cosmic consciousness (from a physicist's point of view), including my favorite title, *Life is Beautiful*. Whew. (I'm coming back as oldest son in a Sicilian family.)

Salvatore will publish a book on Laser technology that only scientists—and our mother—can understand. All of my siblings and their offspring thrive. We are blessed. Or maybe there is something to be said about having the meanest Dad in the whole wide world and an abiding Mom. I would not put it to the test, however.

The Casper the Friendly Ghost Dad of my dream, who belied the hard, tough as nails Dad, was some persona that was always there. What I loved about my father was his rock-solid convictions and that he didn't mince words. Even when I disagreed with his words and convictions, even when I thought he was too rigid, too binary. He laid his cards on the table. Yet he could melt to tears like a woman. Once when I was a teen and had just been handed the astronomical repair bill for my jalopy of a car, by a "family friend," I ran up to my bedroom to cry alone. My father perceived my despair and climbed the stairs to cry with me.

His humanity was all *too* clear to me after a while. After my father had stopped drinking he admitted to my mother that he had had an affair. This admission came some twenty-five years after the fact. My mother's anguish went on for years, especially because she *knew* at the time that he was cheating but preferred to remain in denial (to not experience "buyer's remorse"). She was pregnant with Grace, number six. Dad tended bar at the corner gin joint nights after working all day in the post office. We needed the money. Mary, a barfly, was available for adulterous escapades. Even when she found panties in the car and he had some lame excuse, even when her own mother who lived above them told her *he's fooling around*, my mother, strong in ways I will never know, held her "safe" ground. She got down on her knees one night and cried and prayed to the Blessed Virgin Mary, please banish these terrible suspicious thoughts. And the BVM must have done so.

By the time I learned of my father's infidelity, I had formed mostly negative opinions about, not marriage per se, but about the merits of nuclear family. I can be moved to tears at the image of my mother's suffering, down on her knees begging to be cured of her own sentience and prescience. But for better or worse, I identified with the infidel. My response was something like *only one infidelity in more than fifty years, what's the big deal.* There but for the grace of my many gods went I.

255

When after some twenty years of marriage, my sister Terry's husband had another woman, I was more reactive. I wanted to round up Terry's five sisters and have us go knock on her door. Talk about "mafia tactics"—we'd *tawk* nice at first, but not for long. Grace would hold her back. Tina would talk her mother-tongue circles as a form of (Geneva Conference) acceptable torture. Lisa would cry incessantly and make her feel really bad. Donna would ask open-ended questions that sounded like Zen koans. I might pull her hair. I was outraged. I ended up just calling her and asking through clenched teeth what was she thinking, they had five kids, and other rational questions for an irrational situation. And yes, we had a few pow-wows with our beloved brother-in-law. That *other woman* ended up being a mere catalyst for change in Terry's marriage.

I forgive you
God forgives you
You have to forgive you

On my father's deathbed I don't know how many times he heard Mom's mantra, as his guilt, or fear of hell, would not release its grip and he'd badger her over and over for forgiveness. Just wanting peace in her life, she seemed resigned to accepting that the defendant suffered more than the plaintiff.

Losing my long relationship with Dan, the guy who couldn't or wouldn't dance, aggrieved me—and him—deeply. Not sharing trips to the wilderness in which I had been transformed watching him be transformed, doing his style of dance, as he was enraptured in nature's mystical, liquid currency, was a death best experienced far away in the southern hemisphere. But I had to dance. Like Zelda. They haven't *put me away* yet. While I was still living in Buenos Aires, Dan visited and we shared a trip to Patagonia, the ends of the earth where the wind whistles like the devil or an angry god atop Olympus. It would be our last wild foray after the tumult of parting ways. Yet something better and wonderful would blow our way. I can only sum it up as romantic love flowing into platonic love.

There is a death, a letting go of the concept of a person as love object belonging to you. Love is not subject to gravity, can be neither created nor destroyed. It is a verb, an energy, a force of nature, a wild child, a dynamic entity, ever in flux. When not frozen in artifice, it flows up through all seven chakras, the energy centers along the spine that the sages rave about, from the lowest sexual one to the highest divine. This is the full orgasm. Anyway, that's how I look at and feel it. With this new sort of love, I watched Dan find happiness with another woman and he watched me become the happiest tango bum on the gods' green Earth.

One final footnote: As for Chuck, while I was away those few years in Argentina, he finally convinced Tom to abandon his sartorial concerns and join him on a backpack trip through the infamous Rae Lakes out of

257

Kings Canyon National Park. Sal and his son, Zachary, decided to join the boys. They excitedly planned for their first wilderness trip together, buying the best lightweight gear that sports equipment stores—REI, Marmot, Sports Chalet, Sports Basement—had to offer. Not since long hot summers in Rahway, New Jersey, had Chuck and Sal tromped together through the woods. Since Chuck had the backwoods experience out west, they let him set the pace and so they learned. The hard way. They christened him Trail Guerilla (really Trail Nazi. But let's forsake that awful hyperbolic epithet). Tom took a few videos of them in their forced march that had the tone of a land survey: *now we are crossing Woods Creek, now we are at Vidette Meadow, now almost to Junction Meadow* . . . Not one of them ever went with Chuck again—but I have. Perhaps I better appreciate how wilderness, even its rigors, especially its challenges is so close to home.

20

The Boogie Woogie Man of Chateau Mcely, 2015

RAHWAY, NEW JERSEY Through the 1950s and '60s, twelve of us, two parents and ten kids, squeezed under the pitched roof of a shoebox-sized home. They called our dwelling, too poetically, a Cape Cod. It had the requisite steep roof (or lid) but no gables, just two attic-like dormers in which three girls and three boys were respectively stored. The four youngest were stacked two to a level in bunks in a room next to our parents' bedroom—whose biggest luxury was a door, second biggest being an extra half bathroom.

But hey, it was already twice the size of our first home at 714 Van Buren Avenue, Elizabeth, New Jersey. That's where the first seven kids were born with Mom's parents living upstairs from us. I cherish my memories of climbing the stairs to Grandma Cats' (or Catalano, née Franciamore) who nurtured my mornings with hunks of Italian bread smeared with sweet whipped butter dunked into bowls of milky-sweet coffee. Grandma and Grandpa who never relinquished the fear of poverty that traveled with them from Sicily, didn't give Mom and Dad a break on the rent. So my parents found a couple of creative ways to make ends meet. A certain "Uncle Joe" used to come by on Sundays and tie up our phone for hours.

Years later Mom told me he was a numbers runner who paid for use of the phone. More savory was the homemade pizzas Mom and Dad would make together— always the thick crust Sicilian style. Someone picked up the pizza pies and delivered them around for a good price. If my father had been more grounded and less beleaguered by his demons, my parents could have run a successful restaurant.

Instead they raised kids. When we moved to Rahway, where the last three babies came, it was a little farther from the fumes and smoke stacks of industry and the house was bigger than a bread box but still tight.

Today we look back in amazement at how efficiently our parents managed a brood of so many in those thousand square feet. We all entered the marketplace and flourished. Each and every one of us demanded a ratio of no more than two persons to a bathroom. We demanded something we knew but little of growing up: abundant *personal space*.

Not one of us has fulfilled that desire better than our oldest brother, Jim, who owns a twenty-three room castle outside of Prague, in sleepy Mcely (muh-sell-ee). This past spring, Jim invited his six sisters to come stay in Chateau Mcely, which he and his wife, Inez, run as one of Europe's boutique hotels. Four of us—Terry, Tina, Donna, and I—could make the trip.

For three nights and four days, we would live a fairytale beyond anything our humble roots let us imagine. A driver, who spoke only Czech but who played strikingly

familiar American oldies, picked us up at the Prague
airport. We drifted through magically opening iron gates,
then through the carved wooden doors of the chateau
into a marble and crystal lobby. There, Jim and Inez
welcomed us with flutes of champagne and an herbal
infusion Inez had crafted.

"I feel like Alice," said Donna quaffing her elixir.

"Indeed," Terry agreed, "We've gone down the rabbit
hole."

"And entered a magical kingdom," said Tina.

"You mean *queen*dom," I said. We noted how the St.
George Forest that wreathed the chateau recalled our
childhood tales that sprang from Bohemia, about tricky
wolves and witty witches, dancing fiddles, clever cobblers,
and enchanted princes.

The magic could have rested in the mere knowledge
that even a thousand years before Christ, inhabitants had
lived here in this basin. Jim and Inez said that nearby you
could see remnants of the ancient Celts. To add
miraculous to magical, Mcely is noted as the site of an
apparition of the Virgin Mary, who, Marian Miracle
Hunters report, appeared to three orphans in 1849. Our
mom, a rosary-wielding, inveterate supplicant of the
Blessed Mother, puts full faith in that report. She and Dad
dispensed medals of Our Lady of Medjugorje, the alleged
Yugoslavian apparition.

However, more moving is my brother's true tale of
loss and love. In 2001, Jim's then wife, Jane, succumbed
to breast cancer at age 46. Jim was grieving her death a

year later when he met Inez, a native Czech, in southern California. Love at first sight is how they still describe their magnetism, destined to birth Julia, now nine, and the sumptuous (Europe's greenest) castle. Inez had just purchased the ghostly remains when they met. Built in 1653, dilapidated and renovated over the centuries, the chateau was in hopeless shambles. Inez had a vision, which Jim shared. Together they revived the historic grounds into a five-star lodging, opening its wrought iron gates in 2006.

Few brothers would go all out for their sisters as Jim did. He instructed his entire staff to spare no frills. Unlike the old days, my sisters and I had our own bedrooms, make that suites, with unique themes—the Orient, Africa, Americas, Princess Nely (aka Julia). My chambers—I pretended the sitting area was for my handmaidens—were easily as large as my San Francisco apartment. Each night chocolates, a plate of pastel-colored macaroons, and a one-page bedtime story appeared on the pillows of our king-size beds. Through my tall window I could see the village of 300 and the steeple of its 16th century Baroque church. Before leaving I'd walk its alleys and ponder the historic buildings and the Brother's–Grimm-like yard ornaments. I loved the quiet village that looked just as I imagined in, say, Hansel and Gretel.

But first, there was pampering to be had, from our skin out and inward. Inez, kind of a wise witch of Bohemia, described the ancient herbal tradition of the Nine Flowers. "Olden-day herbalists collected the midsummer blossoms and steeped them into medicinal teas or virgin oils to make curative balms," she said. Thus she has created her own line of essential oils.

Ceramic pots of these aromatic potions were all around. For days we were fragrant with thyme, lavender, rose and other heavenly scents that we dabbed and smeared over hands, face, body, hair. Using the warmed ointments, Petra, a very sturdy masseuse, "basted" us in vigorous rub downs—soft, medium, or deep she inquired. Deep it was and deep she went, removing knots and spasms, I swear had been lodged in my bones since those claustrophobic days back in New Jersey.

In the chateau's Piano Nobile restaurant surrounded by fresh flower bouquets, leaded crystal, polished silver, and shimmering chandeliers, we fattened up on Chef Honza Štěrba's haute cuisine. We adored the delicate bone china on which it was served, a far cry from the Melmac (bounces when dropped) of our youth. Honza's creations could have filled the harvest table of those olden tales—squab in a tangy reduction sauce, red beet mousse, velvety potage of wild mushrooms crowned with crème fraîche, succulent venison, roasted goat cheese salad, and the finest wines, including Bohemian and Moravian vintages. One dessert, chocolate truffles submerged in crème anglaise in a brandy snifter laced with cigar smoke, was wildly imaginative and decadent.

As I've said before, whenever we travel together, my sisters and I morph into what I call a *sister-pede*, one body with twelve legs. As if to recreate the crowded quarters in which we were bred, we shrink the space between us—perhaps psychically as well as physically. We laugh, joke, tease, wave arms, slap backs, talk over each other, get loud and silly. We recalled how in New Orleans our silliness incurred the wrath of Voodoo Priestess Miriam, while in Cuba, Delmis, a Santeria devotee, spontaneously anointed us with Orisha names to calm us down.

Inez, with her native sense of natural healing, guided our tranquility on a stroll through the forest. We have a marked appreciation for fresh air, having grown up in smelling distance of Esso refinery. We ravenously filled our lungs with the earthy spice of beech trees and noble pines. Inez said to keep an eye out for wild boar, which are generally shy. It reminded me how Prince Hugo Maxmilian of the Thurn-Taxis family who owned the chateau until 1948, liked to hunt with hounds (he also like to revel in decadence with dancers and actresses).

The next day, a late-spring snowstorm turned the English gardens with its oaks and linden trees into a white wonderland. It melted quickly and the daffodils and other blooms bounced back, each seasonal display like a stanza in a romantic poem. We explored the knolls and rolling hillside strewn with evocative sculptures, including a moss-eaten mascot, Virgin Mary, the site of Marion pilgrims. Julinka's cottage and a playful witch's lair attested to the chateau's family-friendly atmosphere, that Jim, Inez, and Julia all cultivate. We passed the fanciful Fountain of Fulfilled wishes whose nighttime waters glow violet for the "flow of positive healing energy between the heavens and earth," said Inez.

Eloise at the Plaza had nothing on the *Cusumano sisters at Mcely.* We had the run of the castle with other guests either having checked out or hiding from a sister-pede. Jim and Inez, who live at the chateau on weekends, had returned to their Prague apartment so Julia could attend classes. Down beautifully appointed corridors we explored, the furnishings leaving us breathless. We lingered over precious details—a silver samovar in the tea room, a preening peacock fashioned in dazzling shades of blue gems, a Delft urn, hand-stitched floral designs on satin pillows, velvet sofas, china closets with Inez's herbalist tools on display.

The Gold Room with soft northern light pouring in inspired a session of yoga. I adjusted the sisters' postures as they slipped into warrior poses, downward dog, and triangle pose. We became silent, feeling our flowing chi and something even greater, perhaps the cosmic consciousness that Jim had written about from a physicist point of view in one of his books. I know we all felt the inner light and the rush of endorphins from a mix of body-cleansing *asanas*, and the sisterly reunion. The coddling extravagance was merely icing on the cake. There was something else going on. The Buddhists call it "sympathetic joy." We were not only proud of our brother Jim's ascendancy into hard-earned material wealth, his evolution into spiritual realms, and his finding happiness with Inez and Julia. We were experiencing his joy the same as if it were our own. What happens to one happens to all—suffering and bliss—was a lesson we learned somewhere.

There in the quiet Gold Room, I blurted out, "This is truly transcendent!" But little did I know the best was yet to come.

On the third floor, we climbed the spiral staircase to the library where Jim, a respected Silicon Valley scientist, keeps a library with numerous volumes on his fields, chemistry and physics, and on his lifelong love of alchemy. From there, we climbed a ladder up the bird's nest to a deck with a telescope for studying the heavens. Gazing at the clouds, forest, village, and gardens, I thought of something Francine Prose wrote about Bohemia in the *New York Times*, "How can a place I've never seen seem so eerily familiar as to inspire discrete tiny jolts of deja vu and nostalgia?"

In my case, the answer might have hid in the *cellar*. On our last evening we found it. The sister-pede inched down the twisting ochre stone stairs to the candle-lit cave of the Alchemist Cellar where wines and liquor are stored. Jim, called a neo-*al*chemist by his friends, has had the stonewalls and vaulted ceiling inscribed with notations for alchemical transformations. I recognized the Latin for the four elements, earth, air, water, fire.

I had read how Sir Isaac Newton believed in alchemy and was deeply engaged in the search for *prima materia*. Until the Holy Roman Catholic church began torturing and murdered such "heretics." Newton destroyed his alchemical research.

However, the magical orb that the sisters all saw at once was there in the cellar. It glowed in the red-orange spectrum, a prism of sacred colors revered by eastern contemplatives. *O Spiritus Mundi!* It reminded me of the *Aleph* by Jorge Luis Borges, his small imaginary sphere that allows one to see the universe in its entirety past, present, and future—eternity in its unadulterated glory: *A Wurlitzer jukebox.*

I neglected to mention that our over-populated Cape Cod had a cellar. By nighttime I was petrified of our cellar, certain the boogie man resided there. He would surely grab my legs from under the stairs where he hid. But other nights the cellar rocked with our happiest memories, our boogie woogie man. Jim, being *numero uno,* got the piano lessons and he has an alter ego, Dino. Dino's various bands jammed down the cellar packed with teenagers singing and dancing like a mini American Bandstand. Mom and Dad would feed the grateful teens the Sicilian pizza that once brought them extra income.

Presently, Donna, the baby, took the lead. "Mics at the ready. Hit B-2."

"Whatchu want?" We all sang.

"Baby I got it," We pushed Aretha's buttons and our soul sister backed us. "Respect" was followed by our performing "At the Hop," "Be-Bop-A-Lula," and "Short Shorts," this last being a remnant of Jim/Dino's secret life. Before his entrepreneurial career in science he was a rock 'n' roller, a Jersey boy, in (among other bands) the Royal Teens. The local paper did a story on Jim back then and called him "Rock-a-

Doc," as he had just taken his first job as a doctor of research with Esso.

Fortunately, the Alchemist Cellar, the only place where smoking is allowed, is soundproof. Upstairs we had behaved like genteel aristocrats wearing glass slippers. Now we got down, making this subterranean refuge shake, rattle, and roll. Probably we looked like a centipede that came apart, doing a death flail of eight limbs.

But we knew how to let the good times roll, recalling how back in 1962, the Royal Teens' follow-up song, "Short Short Twist" was a pick hit of the week on Murray the K's Swingin' Soiree when AM radio ruled the waves. It was a school night but we kids were allowed to stay up late and help call in votes to the station, 1010 WINS New York. We remembered our brother Chuck rocking Tina to sleep to the music so hard he rocked backwards into the Hi-Fi. And the time, baby Donna's crib started smoking with her in it because someone put the lamp bulb too close to the mattress. And the time, Mom said we might have to widen a doorway when Dino had the late singer/football player Rosie Grier came to our teensy home.

Catching my breath, I sat at the bar and looked around at the symbols on the ceiling, thinking how the *prima materia* that alchemists seek was of the spirit world, not of the material world (Newton and many others knew this). It can be the music we are weaned on. It would be trite to simply say *You can take the kids out of New Jersey . . . etc.* . But I have to say, it was exhilarating to sojourn in this once-in-a-lifetime fairy-tale palace and find a wonderful throwback to our shared humble past, and come away wondering what's so bad about humble.

Epilogue

I was finishing up production work on this book, when my mother, Carmela, died at age 93 on November 19th, 2015. It was a peaceful last breath she took, I told friends. Although I thought how "peaceful" and "death" sound so incompatible to my ear. But one can only speak about observations from this side of that final act. And in the last six months or so of her life, suddenly non-ambulatory and faculties failing, she was calm, serene, happy even, almost always completely, admirably in the present moment. She smiled a lot and praised her caregivers. She seemed to be in seventh heaven or that fifth and final stage of dying, labeled serenity or acceptance. It was good for us loved ones to see that in her, because for several years after Dad died in 2004, Mom was often grumpy to sum it up mildly.

I like to think on some level of consciousness she assessed her long life with pride and satisfaction, and knew that her ten children and their families, whom she would soon be leaving behind, had all done well in the life she gave us. Even through her grumpy, complaining years, she never ceased to brag about her children.

The significance of losing your Mother, no matter at what age, is so encompassing it takes a while to sink in and for one to assess the deeper meaning. Losing Dad was sad and sorrowful but losing our Mother, was even more so. How can we ever not think of ourselves as the fruit of her womb?

So what does a big Sicilian family do when their Mama leaves their world? They start recalling how she nurtured them with her love of food and cooking for family and friends. Not even a week after Mom's death we all agreed to publish a cookbook Mom had written for us in her eighties, *La Cucina di Carmela*. We combed through her recipes and all of us added stories about Mom and her cooking. The cookbook is a historical family record in a way and also a symbolic act of prolonging the maternal nurturance, something that has no equal. It has been a family project and we are happy to share it with the world.

74732359R00163

Made in the USA
Columbia, SC
05 August 2017